a beautiful bowl of soup

a beautiful bowl of soup

the best vegetarian recipes

by **Paulette Mitchell**

Photographs by **William Meppem**

CHRONICLE BOOKS

SAN FRANCISCO

Library of Congress Cataloging-in-Publication Data:

Mitchell, Paulette.

A beautiful bowl of soup : the best vegetarian recipes /

by Paulette Mitchell ; photographs by William Meppem.

p. cm.

Includes bibliographical references and index.

ISBN 0-8118-3528-6 (Paperback)

1. Soups. 2. Vegetarian cookery. I. Title.

TX757.M59 2004

641.8'13—dc21

2003008519

Manufactured in China.

Design by Azi Rad

Food and prop styling by Andy Harris

Distributed in Canada by Raincoast Books

9050 Shaughnessy Street

Vancouver, British Columbia V6P 6E5

10 9 8 7 6 5 4 3 2

Chronicle Books LLC

85 Second Street

San Francisco, California 94105

www.chroniclebooks.com

Tabasco Sauce is a registered trademark of McIlhenny Co.

acknowledgments and dedication

This cookbook is a result of the talents and dedicated work of many special people. My most sincere thanks to:

Bill LeBlond, editorial director of cookbooks at Chronicle Books, for valuing my talents; to Amy Treadwell, his assistant, for her attention to detail; and to Holly Barrows for filling in during the final phases.

Jane Dystel, my agent, for her wisdom and sound advice.

Photographer William Meppem, for bringing my recipes to life on these pages, and to Azi Rad for creating a pleasing design, to Steve Kim for coordinating the production tasks, and to Jan Hughes, Doug Ogan, and Carolyn Miller, for skillfully seeing this book through editorial.

Brett Mitchell, my son and skilled taster, who misses home-cooked and artistically presented meals while away at college.

And to many friends who tested, tasted, and shared their thoughts: Darryl Trones, Barb Kennedy, Raghavan Iyer, Nathan Fong, Cynthia Myntti, Fran Lebahn, Marie Wintergerst, Emilie Richardson, Connie Reider, Beth Dooley, Loretta McCarthy, Kris Igo, Marcia Rogers, Linda Platt, Stephanie Grossman, Deb Dresler, Lis Viehweg, Gale and Susie Smieja, John Davidson, Tom Nugent, David Briscoe, Jack Balasa, and Tom McNamee.

Finally, I thank every one of my cooking class students, culinary colleagues, and fans who make it possible for me to do what I love doing most — teach, communicate, and share delicious food.

contents

Beautiful soup, so rich and green

Waiting in a hot tureen!

Who for such dainties would not stoop?

Soup of the evening, beautiful soup!

Beautiful soup! Who cares for fish,

Game, or any other dish?

Who would not give all else for two

Pennyworth only of beautiful soup!

—Lewis Carroll

introduction

When I was a girl, my mom made soup every Friday afternoon. Its aroma welcomed me through the back door, ushering in the slower, longed-for weekend, promising a simple, casual family meal. Today, soup transports me to a cozy dinner after a busy workday—and on weekends provides a laid-back meal or elegant do-ahead dinner for friends.

As a chef and mother of a growing teenaged son, I've found myself adapting traditional recipes to our lives today. We still long for the old-fashioned hearty, soul-soothing soups like the ones my mom made, but we're replacing the meat with vegetables, and cutting back on fat while adding the vibrant flavors and aromas of fresh herbs. These are substantial and healthful changes that appeal to everyone, vegetarian or not.

The most indispensable ingredient of all good home cooking:

love for those you are cooking for.

—Sophia Loren

Soups cross international borders, offering a glimpse into the world's cuisines. They make use of indigenous ingredients and offer a range of flavors from Mexico to Japan. In my travels through Europe, Mexico, and the South Pacific, I've found vegetarian soups to be varied and interesting, satisfying and unique. The recipes here are culled from the classics and inspired by recent journeys. Here is minestrone from Siena (page 92), so thick with vegetables you'll need a fork to eat it; a luscious French vegetable soup topped with sherried mushrooms (page 50) that conjures a shopping spree and lunch on the Champs Elysée; and a Mexican soup that begs for crispy tortillas (page 76).

Soup making is one of the most flexible, personal, and enjoyable of kitchen tasks, relying as much on the cook's style and seasonal ingredients as a particular recipe. The range is endless, the work simple. Many a family meal can be easily cooked up in no time. For both casual and elegant entertaining, soup provides glorious possibilities.

Cooking is like love. It should be entered into with abandon or not at all.
—Harriet Van Horne

The preparation of soup requires no fancy equipment, tricky skills, or time-consuming techniques. Most can be made ahead (in fact, many improve when their seasonings have time to marry). And they require only a few moments to assemble before serving. Soups themselves can be the main event, or the freedom they provide can allow you to prepare other courses and, perhaps more importantly, to mingle with your guests. Most soup recipes multiply nicely for a crowd, and as a bonus, leftovers make great lunches and snacks.

TIP

If you double a recipe, do not double the amount of herbs or spices. Use just a little more than in the original recipe, then add more to taste.

Homey though it may be, no soup should be ordinary. Soup making can bring out the artist in you as you garnish and adorn your soups with artistic flair. Here you'll find standout presentations, as well as unique accompaniments, garnishes, and toppings that offer multidimensional flavor in addition to visual appeal. Pumpkin Stew is baked in a pumpkin (page 96); classic caramelized onion soup is updated with goat cheese croutons (page 78); spicy Sweet Potato–Ancho Bisque is swirled with a bright Roasted Red Pepper Cream (page 44), meant to chase away the winter chills. Elegant Pear and Gouda Soup with Toasted Walnut-Cranberry Salsa (page 46) begins a special dinner; Black Bean Soup with Mango Salsa (page 58) packs a pretty, flavorful punch. Lest you think soup is confined to cold weather, Fresh Pink Peach Soup (page 140) soothes and refreshes on a blasting July day. Soup need not be relegated to first course or entrée; you'll also find luscious dessert soups, such as Berry-Wine Soup (page 137) or Strawberry Bonbon Soup (page 141).

A soup may be any combination of ingredients cooked in a liquid and can be thick like a gumbo or thin like a consommé, smooth and creamy like a bisque or chunky like a chowder. Soups may begin a meal or become one. Some are hot and some are cold; all require a spoon.

A soup may be stewed, but a stew will never be souped. *Stew* (both verb and noun) describes not only the dish, but the way it is prepared. Stews are a combination of a cooking liquid and the natural juices of the food being cooked on the stove top or in the oven. Since these vegetarian stews don't contain meat, they require less cooking time than traditional stews. It usually takes less than an hour to bring out the rich flavors of vegetables. Calling for less liquid than soups, stews are thicker and chunkier. You can eat a stew with a fork. Always served hot, a stew is often spooned over a base of noodles, potatoes, rice, or other grains, making the dish a wholesome main course.

Eating stew in a dream portends a reunion with old friends.
—Ned Ballantyne and Stella Coeli, from *Your Horoscope and Dreams*

I've organized these soups according to texture and appearance, rather than by season or course. Some are as wonderful served chilled as hot, and are so noted. Many double as a first course or an entrée; it's really up to you.

A Beautiful Bowl of Soup includes the basics: equipment, technique, advance preparation, serving suggestions, accompaniments, and garnishes. The recipes are meatless, but will appeal to everyone looking for flavor, texture, color, and style. Vegan recipes are listed on page 15 and noted with the recipes. You'll also find the tips, hints, and kitchen wisdom you'll need to make these recipes work at their best.

These recipes have been personally kitchen tested and are sure to work. They are my favorites, and I hope they will comfort and please your family and guests—and make your time in the kitchen easy, creative, and fun.

Soup's on!

Paulette Mitchell

equipment

Soup making doesn't call for much special equipment. Most average home kitchens will likely already have the necessary utensils.

You do need the right pot. Rather than a stockpot, I like to use a heavy Dutch oven for most soups. Most recipes begin by sautéing ingredients before adding the liquid. The bottom of a Dutch oven provides a large, flat surface that allows vegetables to be cooked in a single layer, and the wide opening makes it easy to add ingredients and to check them as they cook. You'll need a tight-fitting lid so that the liquid won't evaporate later in the cooking process as the soup simmers.

Heat-sensitive soups containing ingredients that scorch easily (such as a dessert soup containing chocolate) are best cooked in a double boiler. Be sure to have several long-handled stirring spoons, a large slotted spoon, and, of course, a soup ladle.

I'd be lost without two electrical appliances: a food processor for chopping vegetables and a blender for puréeing smooth, creamy soups. You'll need several sizes of rubber spatulas for scraping food from containers, and large bowls for holding puréed soups, as well as small bowls for assembling ingredients.

Don't underestimate the importance of a good set of knives. If you were to choose just three, I'd recommend a chef's knife in a length that is comfortable for you to handle, a paring knife, and a serrated bread knife. For a cutting surface, select a large cutting board.

As for other equipment, you'll need a vegetable peeler and a grater, basting brushes, whisks, tongs, measuring cups and spoons, a baking sheet or two, a strainer, a colander, and a timer. While it's best to time your cooking by the appearance and aroma of the cooking ingredients, a timer will serve as a reminder to help prevent overcooking.

It's important to have a good-quality peppermill and a zester, and it's fun to have a plastic squeeze bottle for adding creamy toppings to the surface of some soups. You can make an attractive presentation for creamy soups by adding swirls or dots of smooth-textured, brightly colored garnishes.

TIP

To make a "spider web" design on the surface of a creamy soup, drizzle a smooth, creamy garnish in concentric circles, then draw a knife from the center outward, like spokes in a wheel.

Since soups are often made in advance and most leftovers keep well, you'll want storage containers in several sizes. Refrigerate the soup and toppings separately (be sure to label and date containers). Reheat the soup on the stove or in the microwave before serving.

I prefer serving my soups within a few days after they are made instead of freezing them, but many of these soups freeze well (see Tip, page 25). If you plan to freeze, be sure to have a set of freezer containers, too.

ingredients

The vibrant flavors of the soups in this book rely on fresh ingredients and seasonal produce. I've provided alternatives when appropriate. When it comes to tomatoes, for example, canned are often a better choice than flavorless unripe tomatoes. Some vegetables, such as corn and peas, are acceptable in their frozen forms; others, such as chestnuts and beans, can come from a can. While I generally prefer fresh herbs, I've provided the conversion to dried herbs when applicable.

TIPS

Fresh herbs, which come from the leafy part of plants, contain more moisture and therefore are milder than dried herbs. When substituting, use 3 to 4 times more fresh herbs than dried herbs.

Stock up on onions (I prefer yellow for general use) and garlic, to use generously and often.

It's probably illegal to make soups, stews, and casseroles without plenty of onions.

—Maggie Waldron

These recipes call for salt and pepper to be added "to taste." The amount will be determined by personal preference and whether you use salted or unsalted vegetable stock. I find that I use more salt in my soups than in other dishes, and I prefer to cook with *sel gris* (see Tip, page 12).

When seasoning a soup, keep in mind the garnish or topping. Feta and Parmesan cheese, for instance, are very salty. Miso and soy sauce also add saltiness; if you prefer, use a low-sodium soy sauce.

Sea salt, made from evaporated sea water, is available in many supermarkets and natural-foods stores; it can be used just like ordinary table salt. This type of salt includes several naturally present trace minerals, such as iodine, magnesium, and potassium, which give it a fresher, lighter flavor than table salt. Coarse sea salt can be finely ground in a salt mill for use in recipes or at the table. (Make sure that the salt mill has a stainless steel or other noncorrosive mechanism.) Specialty varieties of sea salt include *sel gris,* gray in color and slightly moist, which can be used to season foods while cooking, and *fleur de sel,* used to add flavor at the table. You'll find these in gourmet shops.

You may vary the richness or calorie content of a soup by altering the dairy product you choose, from heavy cream to skim milk, regular sour cream to nonfat sour cream. Take into account the other dishes in your menu and the dietary preferences of your guests. Some light, creamy-textured soups are simply thickened with vegetables.

Sherry and wine make lovely, aromatic additions to elegant soups. Never cook with a wine that you wouldn't drink, but it doesn't have to be the best. I keep on hand 6-ounce bottles of Chardonnay and Cabernet Sauvignon, which are found in most liquor stores. They are ideal for soups. I always keep dry sherry in the refrigerator, where it will retain a quality suitable for cooking for up to 1 month, so I can effortlessly add sophistication to soups. Avoid cooking wines and sherries; they're too salty.

Soup making is not an exact science. As you work with these recipes, you'll become comfortable making alterations such as substituting or adding vegetables you may have on hand, or using more or less of an ingredient, especially those that add spiciness. It's always possible to improvise: To make soups thinner, add more liquid; to thicken them, simmer them longer or without a lid.

techniques

Soup making requires few techniques, making these recipes accessible for even the novice cook.

I was 32 when I started cooking. Up until then, I just ate.
—Julia Child

Begin with *mise en place:* everything in its place, ingredients ready to go when they are needed. Think of steps that may be executed simultaneously: Prepare the garnish while the soup simmers; cook a stew while preparing the accompanying noodles or grain.

Timing and temperature may vary by stove and pan. Judge doneness by appearance, texture, aroma, and flavor.

The first step often is cooking onion and garlic gently in a little butter or oil. This lays the base for flavor. Don't let garlic become brown, or it will be bitter.

For the best flavors, fresh and dried herbs may need to be added at different times in the cooking procedures, as noted. Dried herbs require time to hydrate. Robust fresh herbs, such as rosemary (see Tips, page 115), are added early in the cooking period; tender fresh herbs are added toward the end, as their flavors dissipate with heat. Fresh herbs also may be sprinkled on the top of the completed dish.

Simmer is a key term. First you bring the soup to a boil, then reduce the heat so it bubbles very gently. The stove setting will vary depending on your pan and burner. Just be certain the temperature is constant and kept low enough so that tiny bubbles begin to break the liquid's surface. This allows the ingredients to cook without breaking apart while the flavors blend. When simmering, keep the pan tightly covered, except for occasional stirring, to prevent the soup liquid from boiling away.

Some soups may be partially made, refrigerated, and completed just before serving. This is especially true for warm soups containing dairy products. To retain their smooth texture, avoid boiling these soups when both cooking and reheating.

Tasting is very important to the preparation of any good soup. Always adjust spiciness and saltiness to suit your taste.

The recipes in this book have been well tested to guarantee your success, but don't feel constrained to follow them exactly. You can also omit or interchange the toppings. Trust your palate, and you will be recognized for your homemade soups.

serving soups

When serving guests, it's fun to ladle soup from a large tureen at the table. But it doesn't need to be a conventional tureen. In the summer, use a large pitcher to pour chilled melon soup. Come fall, serve hearty soups from a hollowed-out pumpkin.

Small soup cups or tiny bowls are just right for first-course soups. Mugs are great for sipping creamy soups. Most rimmed soup plates hold generous servings and are ideal for main-course soups. Deep bowls help to retain warmth. Wide, shallow soup plates prevent chunky garnishes from sinking beneath the soup's surface. "Bread bowls," or hollowed-out loaves of fresh baked bread, make wonderful edible containers, as do colorful bell peppers, seeded and scooped clean with a sharp knife and the bottoms trimmed so they'll stand up straight. Or, roast acorn squash (see page 152); they make a lovely presentation and are luscious when scraped up with spoonfuls of soup.

Serve hot soups really hot and chilled soups cold. Heat or refrigerate the bowls to maintain the perfect temperature and to show your guests that you care. And, although they may be considered optional, garnishes add color, texture, and flavor to your soups, as well as style to their presentation.

Never place soup cups or bowls directly on the table, but on a flat plate, which provides a resting place for the spoon when it's not being used.

Don't overlook the importance of spoons. A cup-sized serving of a smooth, creamy soup can be served with a teaspoon. For chunky soups, I like to use large soup spoons. Besides serving the function of holding sizable pieces of vegetables, they simply look and feel substantial.

I've provided recipe yields giving both total cups and approximate numbers of servings. As a rule of thumb, allow $1/2$ to $3/4$ cup of soup for an appetizer or first-course serving. For a main course, allow 1 to 2 cups. Of course, it all depends on what else is served and the richness of the soup.

Soups make a statement, so don't feel as though you are serving "just soup." Whether the event is formal, casual, or somewhere in between, set your table with style. Use interesting dishes, silverware, and bread baskets. For a centerpiece, it's fun to assemble a bowl of the fruits or vegetables used in the soups.

At the table one never grows old.
—Italian proverb

vegan recipes

The recipes in this book are meatless and many are also vegan, or not made with animal-derived foods, including dairy products (butter, cheese, milk) and eggs. These recipes are identified as such before the headnote. Below is a list of the vegan recipes in this book.

In some cases, there is a simple way to make some of the other recipes fit into the vegan category, such as by eliminating a dairy garnish. These alterations are noted with the recipes.

Recipes that call for dairy milk, half-and-half, or cream may be made vegan by substituting soy milk (sometimes labeled "soy beverage" or "soy drink"). This is also a way to prepare some of the soup recipes for those who are lactose intolerant or allergic to milk. Be sure to purchase plain, rather than vanilla, soy milk. Be aware that the flavor will be sweeter than when a soup is made with cow's milk. The appearance also may be different, since some soy milks are not pure white in color. (It may also be necessary to cook with oil rather than butter in order to make these recipes vegan.)

Also, please note that some breads, tortillas, and pitas may contain milk or egg products, so it is recommended that you read the fine print on their ingredient labels.

list of vegan recipes if modified

paulette's tips

These Tips, which you will find with the recipes, will answer questions you may have about selecting, storing, and making the most of the ingredients, as well as the how-to's for several techniques.

vegetable stock basics

It doesn't matter what it's called—stock, bouillon, or broth—the brew provides the medium (flavor and liquid) for a soup. When making vegetarian soups, top-quality ingredients are essential. For preparing recipes in this book, a good vegetable stock is absolutely vital, especially in brothy soups of vegetables and herbs.

Making stock from scratch isn't always practical, so it's important to have good-tasting packaged stocks on hand. You'll find these products in your supermarket or at a natural-foods store.

I've cooked with many vegetable stock products: liquid stock in cans or in aseptic boxes, as well as cubes, granules, and concentrates to mix with water. The choices are endless, and the quality and flavors differ significantly among brands. Experiment to find those you like. In the process, remember that if a vegetable stock is too strongly flavored, use less, or dilute it with water.

Some stocks contain preservatives or sweetener; others are made from organic vegetables. Some are overly salty, some herb flavored, others mild. They may be made of dehydrated vegetables or offer distinct flavors, such as vegetarian "mock chicken" stock. They may be inexpensive or very costly. No matter which you choose, check the package labels and read the small print so you know what is in the product you select and how to store it.

I favor a light-colored unsalted stock powder made from dehydrated vegetables without predominate flavorings to compete with the seasoning in my soups. The powder keeps indefinitely in my kitchen cabinet. I also use liquid stock in aseptic packaging, which offers fresh flavor and long shelf life without the addition of preservatives.

When time permits, preparing vegetable stock is so simple, you don't really need a recipe. Make your stockpot the destination for the odds and ends of many vegetables. Just toss them into a plastic bag in your freezer, where you can store them until needed.

to achieve a balance of flavors, keep the following in mind:

:For light-colored stock, use light-colored vegetables, such as celery stalks (with leaves), leeks, onions, carrots, garlic, and fresh flat-leaf parsley.

:For a darker stock, add to the above lentils, mushrooms, and onion skins. Or, begin by browning the onions and add a dash of soy sauce to the completed stock.

:Strong-flavored vegetables, such as asparagus, bell peppers, broccoli, Brussels sprouts, cabbage, and cauliflower, yield a strong broth. Add them sparingly.

:Parsnips and carrots sweeten the liquid; carrot greens can make a stock bitter.

:Starchy ingredients, such as corn, peas, rice, potatoes, and lentils, will make a stock cloudy if used in abundance.

:If you see foam on the surface of the stock as it cooks, skim it off occasionally to help keep the stock clear.

:Add herbs in moderation. The primary flavorings should come from the main ingredients in the soup recipe; salt and pepper are added to suit your taste after the soup is cooked.

:It is not necessary to peel vegetables. Wash them and trim to remove any bad spots or bruises.

:Cut the vegetables into large chunks. Small pieces disintegrate, making the stock cloudy.

:To intensify the flavors, sauté the vegetables in a small amount of butter or oil before adding the water, or roast the vegetables (see Variation, page 21). You can use a flavorless oil, like canola, or choose olive oil to add its distinctive character.

:Cover the vegetables completely with water and bring to a boil in a stockpot over high heat. Reduce the heat; cover and simmer gently for about 1 hour. (To intensify the flavor, reduce the stock by simmering it, uncovered, for an additional 20 minutes or so.) If the stock remains at a vigorous boil, it will become murky.

:After simmering, drain the stock through a fine-meshed sieve to remove vegetable particles. Lining the sieve with a double layer of cheesecloth will make the broth clearer.

:The stock will keep for up to 3 days in a covered container in the refrigerator, or it can be frozen for up to 6 months. If you plan to use the stock in small amounts, freeze it in ice-cube trays; once frozen, store the cubes in freezer bags.

vegetable stock

Vegan recipe

Here is a basic vegetable stock recipe to get you started.

Heat the oil in a Dutch oven over medium heat. Add the onion, tomato, carrots, celery, leeks, parsnip, and garlic. Cook, stirring occasionally, until the vegetables are tender, 10 to 15 minutes. Add the remaining ingredients. Increase the heat to high and bring to a boil. Reduce the heat; cover and simmer for 1 hour. **Remove the pan** from the heat and let the stock come to room temperature. Drain the stock through a fine-meshed sieve into a large bowl, pressing against the solids with the back of a spoon to extract all the liquid. Discard the solids.

advance preparation

This stock will keep for up to 3 days in a covered container in the refrigerator, or it can be frozen for up to 6 months.

variation

For a richer stock, first roast the vegetables until they caramelize before adding them to the pot: Preheat the oven to 425° F. Toss the vegetables with the oil until coated. Transfer the vegetables to a roasting pan or spread them on a jelly-roll pan lined with aluminum foil. Bake, uncovered, turning the vegetables occasionally, for about 30 minutes, or until tender and browned. Transfer the roasted vegetables to a Dutch oven; add the remaining ingredients and follow the vegetable stock recipe.

In the childhood memories of every good cook, there's a large kitchen, a simmering pot, and a mom.

—Barbara Costikyon

2 tablespoons canola or olive oil

1 large onion, cut into 1-inch chunks

1 large tomato, quartered

2 large carrots, cut into 1-inch chunks

2 celery stalks, cut into 1-inch chunks, with leaves

2 leeks (white parts only), halved lengthwise, rinsed, and cut into 1-inch slices

1 parsnip, cut into 1-inch chunks

4 cloves garlic, sliced in half crosswise

8 cups water

4 sprigs fresh flat-leaf parsley

2 sprigs fresh thyme

2 sprigs fresh basil

2 bay leaves

6 whole black peppercorns

Makes 8 cups

creamy soups

Velvety cream soups are simple luxuries. The sensuous texture may be achieved in various ways. Roux, a cooked mixture of flour and butter to which cream or milk is added, is the traditional thickener for creamy soups, as in Pear and Gouda Soup with Toasted Walnut–Cranberry Salsa (page 46).

Cooked vegetables, such as potatoes, carrots, or peas, can be puréed to add body to a soup and give it a creamy texture as they do in Curried Carrot Soup with Cilantro-Pistachio Cream (page 26) and Yukon Gold Potato Soup with Black Olive Caviar (page 28). Sometimes, only part of the soup is puréed to thicken a soup filled with chunky ingredients. This is always an option when using puréed creamy soup recipes.

TIP

Brown-skinned russet potatoes are starchier than red-skinned potatoes. They are the potato of choice for thickening soups.

It's important that vegetables be cooked until very tender if they're to be puréed. A blender achieves a smoother consistency, breaking down the fibers of vegetables more effectively than a food processor.

After cooking the vegetables and stock, let them cool for 5 to 10 minutes before blending. Because the volume of the soup is usually larger than the capacity of the blender container, it will be necessary to purée the ingredients in several batches. You'll need a bowl or other container to hold the puréed mixture before it is poured back into the Dutch oven.

Ladle part of the vegetables and some of the vegetable stock into the blender jar, filling it only about a third to half full. Hold a towel over the blender lid as a safety precaution, since some soup may escape. Start with the lowest speed, and pulse the machine in short spurts to begin. Then gradually increase the speed until you reach the desired consistency. Take care not to overprocess; potatoes, in particular, can become gummy if processed for too long.

To use a food processor for puréeing soups, fit it with the metal blade. Ladle some of the cooked vegetables and part of the soup liquid into the food processor bowl. Do not overfill the bowl, or it will overflow when the machine is turned on. Close and pulse the machine several times, then run it without stopping just until the desired texture is reached. You may need to push down the ingredients from the side of the bowl using a rubber spatula to ensure a smooth consistency.

After puréeing the soup, it will need reheating. Rinse the Dutch oven with water and then return the soup to the pot, stirring gently as you add any other ingredients, and reheat the soup to serving temperature.

Handheld blenders, also called immersion or stick blenders, can be lowered directly into a pot of soup. This means less time and less mess, since the soup does not need to be transferred to a blender container. Generally, however, these don't have the power of a traditional blender. To use a handheld blender, hold the machine upright in the center bottom of your pan, then turn it on and move it around but do not bring it to the surface. Keeping the blade in the food will prevent spattering.

Many puréed soups call for the addition of a dairy product. I've suggested the choice or choices I use most often and in the order of my preference, but keep in mind that milk (skim, percent, or whole), half-and-half, and cream are interchangeable in these recipes. Even a sour-cream garnish can be nonfat. Your selection will determine how filling and hearty your soup will be.

If you'd like, you can prepare these soups in advance through the puréeing step and refrigerate or freeze the mixture, then add the dairy product (milk, half-and-half, or cream) when reheating.

The smooth, flat surface of creamy soups offers a perfect canvas for garnishes that add color, texture, flavor, and spice, as well as style. A cream in a contrasting color, such as Roasted Red Pepper Cream (page 44), can be applied in a swirl or design using a plastic squeeze bottle. Toasted Walnut–Cranberry Salsa (page 46) and Sherried Mushrooms (page 50) add flavor and texture. And shaped Buttered Croutons (page 151) can add a touch of whimsy.

TIP

If you want to freeze a soup that includes dairy, prepare it without the dairy product, then freeze it. When you want to serve it, defrost the soup, heat it, and stir in the dairy product. For soups containing pasta, freeze them without the pasta, then stir in the cooked pasta once the soup is defrosted and reheated.

I live on good soup, not fine words.
—Molière

curried carrot soup with cilantro-pistachio cream

This colorful soup makes a satisfying main course or an elegant first course. You may use milk in lieu of half-and-half and add more vegetable stock if you prefer a thinner, lighter soup.

to make the cream

Process all the ingredients, except the half-and-half, in a food processor to make a coarse purée. Add the half-and-half; process until smooth. Set aside to allow the flavors to blend.

to make the soup

Melt the butter in a Dutch oven over medium heat. Add the apple and onion; cook, stirring occasionally, until the onion is translucent, about 5 minutes. Add the curry powder; stir for about 30 seconds.

Add the vegetable stock and carrots. Increase the heat to high and bring to a boil. Reduce the heat; cover and simmer until the carrots are very tender, about 15 minutes.

In 2 batches, purée the soup in a blender until smooth. (The soup will have tiny specks of carrot rather than being completely smooth.)

Return the soup to the pan. Add the half-and-half; stir occasionally over medium heat until warmed through. Season to taste.

Garnish each serving with crème fraîche, a swirl of the cilantro cream, and a sprinkling of chives. (To dispense the cilantro cream in a plastic squeeze bottle, thin it with additional milk or water.)

cream

1	cup loosely packed fresh cilantro leaves *(see Tip)*
1/4	cup salted pistachios
1/4	cup extra-virgin olive oil
2	cloves garlic
1/4	teaspoon freshly ground pepper
1/4	cup half-and-half or milk

soup

2	tablespoons unsalted butter
1	apple, cored, peeled, and coarsely chopped
1	cup coarsely chopped red onion
2	teaspoons curry powder
1 1/2	cups vegetable stock
1	pound (about 5) carrots, cut into 1-inch chunks
1	cup half-and-half or milk
~	salt and freshly ground pepper to taste
~	crème fraîche *(see Tip, page 147)* or sour cream and finely chopped fresh chives for garnish

Makes 4 cups (4 servings)

advance preparation

Refrigerate this soup and the cilantro cream in separate covered containers for up to 3 days. When reheating the soup and before serving the cilantro cream, stir in vegetable stock or milk to thin as desired.

TIP

Cilantro is also known as fresh coriander or Chinese parsley. Ground coriander, an ingredient in most curry powders, is made from the ground seeds of the plant and serves a different purpose in cooking than the fresh leaves.

The only carrots that interest me are the number you get in a diamond.
—Mae West

yukon gold potato soup with black olive caviar

Vegan recipe if olive oil is substituted for the butter and the eggs, sour cream, and crème fraîche are omitted

Yukon Gold potatoes, with their warm, buttery yellow hue, are the perfect background for a showy (and, I think, necessary) topping of crumbled eggs, black olive caviar, and fresh chives.

to make the soup

Melt the butter in a Dutch oven over medium-low heat. Add the onion; cook, stirring occasionally, until tender, about 10 minutes.

Stir in the vegetable stock, potatoes, garlic, salt and pepper. Increase the heat to high and bring to a boil. Reduce the heat; cover and simmer until the potatoes are very tender, about 10 minutes.

to make the caviar

Stir together all the ingredients in a small bowl. Taste and adjust the seasoning.

to complete the recipe

In several batches, purée the soup in a blender until smooth. (Take care not to overprocess.)

Return the soup to the pan and stir occasionally over medium heat until serving temperature. Taste and adjust the seasoning.

Garnish each serving with about 2 tablespoons egg, a dollop of sour cream, a small mound of caviar, and a sprinkling of chives and pepper.

continued . . .

soup

3	tablespoons unsalted butter
1	cup coarsely chopped onion
5	cups vegetable stock (use a light-colored stock)
2	Yukon Gold potatoes (about 1 pound total), peeled and cut into 3/4 inch chunks (about 3 cups)
1	clove garlic, coarsely chopped
~	dash of salt and freshly ground pepper, or to taste

caviar

1	cup (4 ounces) pitted black olives, finely chopped
2	tablespoons minced fresh flat-leaf parsley
1	tablespoon extra-virgin olive oil
2	cloves garlic, minced
~	dash of freshly ground pepper, or to taste
~	pinch of red pepper flakes, or to taste

garnishes

2	hard-cooked eggs, finely crumbled *(see Tip, page 30)*
~	sour cream or crème fraîche *(see Tip, page 147),* finely chopped fresh chives, and coarsely ground pepper

Makes 5 cups (4 to 6 servings)

Refrigerate this soup and the caviar in separate covered containers for up to 3 days. When reheating the soup, stir in vegetable stock to thin as desired.

TIP

To hard-cook eggs, place the eggs in a single layer in a saucepan and cover with at least 1 inch of cold water. Cover and bring the water to a full rolling boil over medium-high heat. Remove the pan from the heat and let the eggs stand in the water, covered, for about 15 minutes for large eggs. (For larger or smaller eggs, adjust the time up or down by about 3 minutes for each size variation.) Drain off the hot water and immediately cover the eggs with cold water; let stand until the eggs are completely cool. This cooling process prevents a dark gray-green surface from forming around the yolk. (If it does occur, the greenish color is harmless and does not alter the nutritional value or flavor of the egg.) Quick cooling also causes the eggs to contract, making them easier to peel. Refrigerate hard-cooked eggs for up to 1 week.

I have the simplest tastes. I am always
satisfied with the best.
—Oscar Wilde

cream of tomato soup with Puff Pastry Crowns

I remember grade-school lunchtime, when I would dash from the school bus into my mom's sunny kitchen welcomed by the aroma of tomato soup, which I topped with crumbled saltines. This tomato soup is as comforting as Mom's, but fresh and elegant wearing a pastry crown instead of saltines. To simplify, garnish the soup with dollops of Parmesan Cream (page 40) or Black Olive Caviar (page 28) in place of the crowns.

to make the soup

Wrap the thyme, bay leaf, and peppercorns in a square of cheesecloth and tie with kitchen twine (see Tips, page 33). Set aside.

Melt 2 tablespoons of the butter in a Dutch oven over medium heat. Add the onion; cook, stirring occasionally, until translucent, about 5 minutes.

Whisk together the water and tomato paste in a small bowl; add to the soup. Stir in the tomatoes and garlic; immerse the cheesecloth bag in the soup. Bring to a boil over high heat. Reduce the heat; cover and simmer until the tomatoes are very tender, about 30 minutes.

to make the puff pastry

Preheat the oven to 400° F. Line a baking sheet with parchment paper (see Tips, page 162). Lightly beat the egg with the water. Unroll the puff pastry on a lightly floured board. Cut rounds of puff pastry slightly smaller than the soup bowl tops. (You can use the scraps of dough to make designs, such as an arrangement of triangles, atop the pastry.) Place the rounds on the prepared baking sheet and lightly brush the tops with the egg mixture. Bake for about 15 minutes, or until the dough is puffed and golden brown. Transfer the rounds to a wire rack; set aside to cool.

continued . . .

soup

1	small sprig fresh thyme
1	bay leaf
1	teaspoon whole black peppercorns
4	tablespoons unsalted butter
1	cup finely chopped onion
1	cup water
1/3	cup tomato paste
4	large (2 pounds) ripe tomatoes, peeled and quartered *(see Tips, page 57)*
4	cloves garlic, minced

puff pastry

1	egg
1	tablespoon water
1	frozen puff pastry sheet (8 to 9 ounces), thawed *(see Tips, page 33)*

to complete the recipe

2	cups half-and-half or milk
1	tablespoon packed light brown sugar
1/2	teaspoon salt, or to taste
~	ground white pepper to taste

31

Makes 4 cups (4 servings)

When the tomatoes are tender, remove the cheesecloth bag from the soup. Purée the soup in a blender.

Place a coarse-meshed sieve over a bowl. Pour the soup into the sieve in several batches, stirring with a wooden spoon. Discard the soup solids.

Return the soup to the pan.

to complete the recipe

Add the remaining 2 tablespoons butter, the half-and-half, brown sugar, salt, and pepper. Stir until the butter melts and the soup is heated through. Taste and adjust the seasoning.

Top each serving with a pastry round.

advance preparation

This soup will keep for up to 3 days in a covered container in the refrigerator. The puff pastry is best when baked just before serving.

variation

Top the servings with Buttered Croutons (page 151) rather than puff pastry crowns.

TIPS

Puff pastry is a French pastry made using a method of rolling and folding that encloses butter in pastry layers. When baked, the moisture in the butter creates steam, causing the thin layers of dough to puff and separate into dozens of flaky layers. You can find premade puff pastry sheets in the frozen section of most supermarkets. Thaw at room temperature for 20 to 30 minutes before using. Wrap unused sheets in plastic wrap or foil and return to the freezer.

A bouquet garni is a bunch of herbs either placed in a cheesecloth bag or tied together with kitchen twine. The herbs infuse soups, stews, and broths with their flavors and are then easily removed without leaving a leafy trace.

There is nothing like soup. It is by nature eccentric: no two are ever alike, unless of course you get your soup from cans.
—Laurie Colwin, from *Home Cooking*

roasted butternut squash soup with toasted walnuts

This fragrant, luscious soup invites you to stay in rather than go out on a blustery winter night. I like to serve it with a roasted beet and feta salad on radicchio and baby spinach, drizzled with an olive oil-lemon vinaigrette.

Preheat the oven to 350° F. Line a baking sheet with aluminum foil.

Place the squash segments, skin-side up, on the prepared baking sheet. Surround with the onion and carrots. Brush all the surfaces lightly with olive oil. Gently remove the loose papery skin from the garlic bulb. Trim off the top stem and about 1/4 to 1/2 inch of the garlic bulb, exposing the cloves but leaving them intact; brush lightly with olive oil. Wrap the garlic in aluminum foil and place on the baking sheet.

Roast the vegetables in the center of the oven for about 40 minutes, or until they are very tender. Set aside until the squash and garlic are cool enough to handle.

Squeeze the garlic cloves out of their skins; scrape the flesh from the squash; remove the outer layer from the onion. Add half of the garlic, squash, onion, and carrots to the blender. Add about 1 cup of the vegetable stock and purée until smooth; repeat.

Heat the 1 tablespoon oil in a Dutch oven over medium heat. Add the curry powder; stir for about 30 seconds. Pour the soup into the pan. Stir in the remaining 1 cup stock, the sherry, brown sugar, pepper, oregano, and cinnamon. Cover and simmer, stirring occasionally, for about 10 minutes. Add the milk and stir until heated through. Taste and adjust the seasoning.

Garnish each serving with a dollop of crème fraîche and a sprinkling of nuts and fried sage.

1   butternut squash (about 2 pounds), quartered lengthwise and seeded

1   large yellow onion, peeled and quartered

2   carrots, halved horizontally (also halved vertically if very thick)

~   olive oil for brushing, plus 1 tablespoon olive oil

1   whole garlic bulb

3   cups vegetable stock

1   teaspoon curry powder

1/4 cup dry sherry

1   tablespoon packed light brown sugar *(see Tips)*

1/2 teaspoon freshly ground pepper, or to taste

2   teaspoons minced fresh oregano, or 1/2 teaspoon dried oregano

1/8 teaspoon ground cinnamon, or to taste

1/2 cup milk or half-and-half

~   salt to taste

~   crème fraîche *(see Tip, page 147)* or sour cream, toasted chopped walnuts *(see Tips)*, and Fried Sage *(page 163)* or coarsely chopped fresh flat-leaf parsley for garnish

Makes 5 cups (4 to 6 servings)

advance preparation

This soup will keep for up to 3 days in a covered container in the refrigerator. When reheating, stir in vegetable stock, water, or milk to thin as desired.

variation

Omit the crème fraîche or sour cream and toasted walnuts; garnish the soup with Herbed Garlic Croutons (page 150).

TIPS

Brown sugar is made of white sugar combined with molasses, which gives it a soft texture. It is available in both light and dark varieties; the lighter the color, the milder the flavor. Hardened brown sugar can be softened by placing an apple wedge in the jar or bag of sugar; seal tightly for 1 or 2 days, then remove the apple.

Toasting intensifies the flavor and enhances the texture of most nuts. To toast nuts on the stove top, put them in a single layer in a dry skillet over medium heat. Stir or toss, watching closely, until they are fragrant and golden brown, about 4 minutes. Or, nuts can be toasted on a baking sheet or pie plate in a preheated 350° F oven for 5 to 10 minutes, stirring frequently. To prevent burning, remove the nuts from the skillet or baking pan as soon as they are toasted.

chestnut soup

During the winter months, hot roasted chestnuts are sold by vendors on the boulevards of Paris, and the meaty nut is a popular ingredient in bistros around France. Canned chestnuts, available in many supermarkets and gourmet shops, are as rich and earthy as the fresh. No peeling and fussing, and they're ready in minutes. I like to serve this soup in small cups topped with foamy milk steamed using my cappuccino machine and a sprinkling of freshly grated nutmeg. My friend Barb, who prepares this soup for winter holidays, tops the servings with a fan of paper-thin apple slices.

Melt the butter with the olive oil in a Dutch oven over medium-low heat. Add the carrot, celery, and shallots; cook, stirring occasionally, until the vegetables are very tender, about 10 minutes. Stir in the vegetable stock.

In 2 batches, purée the soup with the chestnuts in a blender until smooth.

Return the soup to the pan. Add the half-and-half and sherry. Stir gently over medium heat until heated through. Season to taste.

Serve the soup, cappuccino style, in soup mugs or small, deep bowls topped with foamy milk. Thinly slice the remaining chestnut and place on the soup. Finish with a dash of nutmeg.

advance preparation

Prepare the soup through the puréeing step; refrigerate in a covered container for up to 3 days. Reheat and add the half-and-half and sherry just before serving.

TIP

Sherry is a fortified wine to which brandy or another spirit has been added to increase the flavor and boost the alcohol content. Sherries vary in color, flavor, and sweetness. Finos are dry and light; they include manzanillas, which are very dry and delicate, with a hint of saltiness, and amontillados, which are aged and have a distinctively nutty flavor. Olorosos, often labeled cream or golden sherry, are darker in color and sweet.

1   tablespoon unsalted butter
1   tablespoon olive oil
1   carrot, finely chopped
1   celery stalk, finely chopped
1/4 cup finely chopped shallots
2   cups vegetable stock
1   10-ounce can peeled chestnuts, drained, reserve 1 chestnut for garnish
1   cup half-and-half or milk
1/4 cup dry sherry (see Tip)
~   salt and freshly ground pepper to taste

~   hot foamy milk, freshly grated nutmeg (see Tips, page 140), and thinly sliced chestnut for garnish

Makes 4 cups (4 to 6 servings)

roasted bell pepper soup with lemon vinaigrette

Vegan recipe if crème fraîche and sour cream garnishes are omitted

Roasting your own bell peppers is the secret to top-notch flavor. Roast the peppers, then prepare the soup in two separate batches. Pour the red and yellow soups into the bowl all at once for an impressive "yin-yang" presentation.

to make the vinaigrette

Whisk together the olive oil and lemon juice in a small bowl. Season to taste. Set aside.

to make the soup

Heat the oil in a Dutch oven over medium heat. Add the potato, onion, carrot, and garlic; cook, stirring occasionally, until the vegetables are crisp-tender, about 10 minutes. Transfer half of the vegetables to a large saucepan.

Stir 2 cups of the vegetable stock into each pan. Coarsely chop the roasted bell peppers. Put the red bell peppers in one pan and the yellow bell peppers in the other. Increase the heat to high under both pans and bring to a boil. Reduce the heat; cover both pans and simmer until the vegetables are very tender, about 10 minutes.

Separately purée the red and yellow bell pepper soups in a blender until smooth. Return the soups to the 2 pans and reheat to serving temperature. Season to taste.

To serve, using 1/2-cup measuring cups, pour both soups into shallow wide bowls in steady streams at the same time for a yin-yang look. Garnish with a drizzle of the vinaigrette, a generous sprinkling of chives, and a large dollop of crème fraîche.

advance preparation

This soup will keep for up to 5 days in 2 separate covered containers (one for the yellow bell pepper soup, the other for the red) in the refrigerator. When

vinaigrette

2 tablespoons extra-virgin olive oil

2 tablespoons fresh lemon juice

~ salt and freshly ground pepper to taste

soup

2 tablespoons olive oil

1 large russet potato (about 12 ounces), peeled and cut into 1/2-inch chunks (about 2 1/4 cups)

1 cup finely chopped onion

1 carrot, finely chopped

2 cloves garlic, minced

4 cups vegetable stock

3 red bell peppers, roasted *(see Tips)*

3 yellow bell peppers, roasted *(see Tips)*

~ salt and freshly ground pepper to taste

~ finely chopped fresh chives *(see Tips)* and crème fraîche *(see Tip, page 147)* or sour cream for garnish

Makes 6 cups (6 servings)

reheating the soups, stir in water to thin as desired. (Or, for a creamy texture, stir in half-and-half or cream.) Refrigerate the vinaigrette in a covered container for up to 2 days.

variations

~ Make the soup with only red or yellow bell peppers, rather than a combination.

~ In a pinch for time? Substitute one 12-ounce jar roasted yellow bell peppers and one 12-ounce jar roasted red bell peppers for the freshly roasted peppers. The jars contain salt, so you'll need to add less to the soup.

~ For garnishing, substitute bottled basil-flavored olive oil for the lemon vinaigrette.

TIPS

To roast bell peppers, preheat the broiler and line a baking sheet with aluminum foil. Remove and discard the stem and cut each bell pepper in half lengthwise; remove and discard the seeds and ribs. Place the pepper halves, skin-side up, in a single layer on the prepared pan; flatten each with the palm of your hand. Lightly brush the skins with olive oil. Broil for about 15 minutes, or until the pepper halves are fork-tender and the skins are blackened and blistered. Transfer the pepper halves to a heavy-duty self-sealing plastic bag or a brown paper bag and seal; set aside until cool, for at least 20 minutes or for up to several hours. (The steam will loosen the skins.) Remove the pepper halves from the bag. Peel the peppers with your hands, using a paring knife to scrape away any peel that doesn't come off easily; discard the skins. Or, whole bell peppers can be roasted on a grill over a hot charcoal fire or over the flame of a gas stove. Remove the stem and seeds before using. Use right away or store the peeled peppers and their juices in a covered container in the refrigerator for up to 1 week.

Chives are members of the onion family. Given a choice, buy potted chives; they are fresher than cut ones. Use scissors to snip off what you need, cutting off whole blades rather than chopping the tops off all the blades. If you buy cut chives, wrap them in a damp paper towel, seal in a plastic bag, and refrigerate for up to 1 week. Add chives to a dish toward the end of the cooking time to help retain their flavor. Do not substitute dried chives for fresh; use the green part of green onions cut into julienne strips instead.

fresh pea soup with parmesan cream

When we think of pea soup, we usually think of a slow-cooked soup made with dried split peas and flavored with ham. This version, made with frozen fresh peas, is smoother in texture and fresher in flavor, and it's much quicker to prepare. Serve with Cheese Sticks (page 160) on the side.

40

to make the cream

Stir together all the ingredients in a small bowl. Taste and adjust the seasoning; set aside.

to make the soup

Heat the oil in a Dutch oven over medium heat. Add the celery, onion, leek, and garlic; cook, stirring occasionally, until the onion is translucent, about 5 minutes.

Stir in the vegetable stock and peas. Increase the heat to high and bring to a boil. Reduce the heat; cover and simmer until the vegetables are very tender, about 5 minutes.

Meanwhile, steam the carrots in a covered steamer over boiling water until tender, about 10 minutes. Or, put the carrots in a small microwave-proof dish and add about 2 tablespoons water. Cover tightly and microwave on high for about 5 minutes. Drain well and set aside.

In several batches, purée the pea mixture and the milk in a blender until smooth.

Return the soup to the pan. Stir in the carrots, sugar, nutmeg, salt, and pepper. Stir gently over medium heat until heated through. Taste and adjust the seasoning.

Top each serving with a dollop of Parmesan Cream and croutons.

cream

1/2 cup sour cream

2 tablespoons freshly grated Parmesan cheese *(see Tips)*

1/4 teaspoon ground white pepper, or to taste

soup

2 tablespoons canola oil

2 celery stalks, finely chopped

1/2 cup finely chopped onion

1 leek (white part only), halved lengthwise, rinsed, and cut into 1/8-inch slices

2 cloves garlic, minced

1 1/2 cups vegetable stock

1 16-ounce bag frozen baby peas *(see Tips)*

2 carrots, cut into 1/8-inch slices

1 1/2 cups milk

2 teaspoons sugar

~ dash of freshly grated nutmeg, *(see Tip, page 140)* or to taste

~ salt and ground white pepper to taste

~ Buttered Croutons *(page 151)* for garnish

Makes 5 cups (4 to 6 servings)

Refrigerate this soup and the Parmesan cream in separate covered containers for up to 3 days. When reheating the soup, stir in milk or vegetable stock to thin as desired.

TIPS

The best-quality Parmesan cheese is Italy's Parmigiano-Reggiano. Aged 3 to 4 years, it has a granular texture and complex flavor compared with domestic varieties, which are aged for only about 1 year. The imported cheese also melts beautifully in soup. Buy Parmesan in blocks and use a hand grater or food processor to grate your own just before using. Or, purchase freshly grated Parmesan at a cheese shop or deli. Sealed in a tightly closed container, grated Parmesan will keep in the refrigerator for up to 1 week. It can be frozen; however, the flavor and texture will deteriorate. Wrapped tightly in plastic wrap and refrigerated, a block of Parmesan will keep for up to 6 weeks.

Generally, the flavor of baby peas, or *petits pois,* is preferable to that of the regular-sized peas. Harvested when young, baby peas remain especially sweet after picking; they also retain a brighter green color and a firmer texture.

curried granny smith **apple and yam soup** with glazed pecans

Vegan recipe if pecans are omitted

Tart apples, a sweet yam, ginger, and curry are the magical components of this soup. In addition to the sweet and salty pecans, top servings with colorful pomegranate seeds if you make this in October, November, or December.

to make the pecans

Preheat the oven to 250° F. Line a jelly-roll pan with aluminum foil and spray it with vegetable-oil cooking spray. Melt the butter in a small nonstick saucepan over medium heat. Stir in the corn syrup, water, and salt. Bring to a boil, stirring constantly. Remove the pan from the heat. Add the pecans and stir until completely coated. Spread the nuts in a single layer on the prepared pan. Bake, stirring occasionally, for about 60 minutes, or until lightly browned and dry. Transfer to a plate and let cool, then coarsely chop. (Whole pecans will sink to the bottom of soup bowls.)

to make the soup

Heat the oil in a Dutch oven over medium heat. Add the carrot, celery, leek, garlic, ginger, and curry powder; cook, stirring occasionally, until the leek is softened, about 5 minutes.

Stir in the vegetable stock, sweet potato, apples, and wine. Increase the heat to high and bring to a boil. Reduce the heat; cover and simmer until the vegetables are very tender, about 25 minutes.

In several batches, purée the soup in a blender until smooth. Return the soup to the pan and reheat to serving temperature. Season to taste.

Garnish each serving with a sprinkling of pecans and pomegranate seeds.

pecans

1	tablespoon unsalted butter
1	tablespoon light corn syrup
2	teaspoons water
1/2	teaspoon salt
1	cup (4 ounces) whole pecans

soup

1	tablespoon canola oil
1	carrot, finely chopped
1	celery stalk, finely chopped
1	leek (white part only), halved lengthwise, rinsed, and cut into 1/4-inch slices
2	cloves garlic, minced
2	teaspoons minced fresh ginger
2	teaspoons curry powder *(see Tips)*
5	cups vegetable stock
1	orange-fleshed sweet potato (about 10 ounces), peeled and cut into 1/2-inch chunks (about 2 cups)
2	Granny Smith or other tart apples, cored, peeled, and cut into 1/2-inch cubes
1/2	cup dry white wine
~	salt and ground white pepper to taste
~	pomegranate seeds *(see Tips)* or dried cranberries for garnish

This soup will keep for up to 3 days in a covered container in the refrigerator. Store the nuts for up to 3 weeks in an airtight container at room temperature.

TIPS

Curry powder, a mixture of many herbs and spices, is blended in literally thousands of versions according to the region of India, traditions, and the tastes of the cook. Standard curry powders are quite mild; imported brands, often called Madras, are usually hotter. To eliminate the raw taste of curry powder, sauté it in butter or oil rather than simply adding it to a dish. Since curry powder quickly loses its pungency, purchase it in small quantities, and store airtight in a dark, dry place for up to 3 months.

Pomegranates yield bright red, sweet, tart, and edible seeds and are available from October through December. They can be refrigerated for up to 2 months. To use, cut the fruit in half and pry out the seeds, removing any light-colored membrane that adheres. To simplify the task and avoid splashes of the juice, submerge each half in a bowl of cold water and tear the flesh apart under water. The seeds will drop to the bottom and the pulp will float. Remove the pulp with a slotted spoon and strain the seeds.

In eating we experience a certain special
and indefinable well-being.
—Jean-Anthelme Brillat-Savarin

sweet potato–ancho bisque
with apple–pecan salsa
and roasted red pepper cream

A dark reddish-brown chili with an earthy sweet flavor and mild heat, anchos are one of the most widely used dried chilies. They are made from the fresh heart-shaped poblano chilies that grow throughout central Mexico. Adjust the amount of jalapeño in the salsa to make the assertiveness of the composed dish just right for you.

to make the soup

Rinse the ancho chilies; put them in a small bowl and cover with hot water (just below the boiling point). Soak until softened, about 20 minutes.

Meanwhile, heat the oil in a Dutch oven over medium-low heat. Add the onion, carrot, and celery; cook, stirring occasionally, until tender, about 10 minutes. Drain the chilies; remove the stems, rinse to remove the seeds, and coarsely chop (see Tip, page 75).

Stir in the vegetable stock, wine (if using), potatoes, and chilies. Increase the heat to high and bring to a boil. Reduce the heat; cover and simmer until the potatoes are very tender, about 10 minutes.

to make the salsa

Stir together all the ingredients in a medium bowl; adjust the seasoning to taste.

to make the cream

Purée the bell pepper and sour cream in a blender; if necessary, stir in milk so the mixture has a cake-batter consistency. Season to taste. Transfer the cream to a plastic squeeze bottle, if available.

When the potatoes are done, purée the soup in several batches in a blender until smooth.

Return the soup to the pan.

soup

2	ancho chilies *(see Tips)*
2	tablespoons olive oil
1/2	cup coarsely chopped onion
1/2	cup coarsely chopped carrot
1/4	cup coarsely chopped celery
6	cups vegetable stock
1/2	cup dry red wine *(optional)*
1	large orange-fleshed sweet potato (about 12 ounces), peeled and cut into 1/2-inch chunks (about 2 1/4 cups)
1	large russet potato (about 12 ounces), peeled and cut into 1/2-inch chunks (about 2 1/4 cups)

salsa

1	cup finely diced Granny Smith apple at room temperature
1/4	cup toasted chopped pecans *(see Tips, page 35)*
2	tablespoons fresh lime juice
1	tablespoon minced fresh cilantro
1	teaspoon minced fresh red jalapeño chili, or to taste

cream

1/2	cup coarsely chopped jarred roasted red bell pepper
1/4	cup sour cream or crème fraîche *(see Tip, page 147)*
~	milk, as needed
~	salt and freshly ground pepper to taste

Makes 8 cups (8 servings)

to complete the recipe

Add the milk and stir occasionally over medium heat until heated through. Season to taste.

Top each serving with a scoop of salsa. Surround with swirls of the cream mixture.

advance preparation

Refrigerate the soup and cream mixture in separate covered containers for up to 3 days. When reheating, stir in vegetable stock or milk to thin as desired. Prepare the salsa just before serving.

variation

Substitute Cilantro-Pistachio Cream (page 26) for the roasted red pepper cream.

TIP

The best dried chilies are sun dried, as stated on the package label; oven drying may make the skins bitter. Dried chilies will keep indefinitely in a tightly closed container in a cool, dry place, out of direct sunlight.

pear and gouda soup with toasted walnut–cranberry salsa

Baby Gouda has a mild, nutlike flavor, and it melts into a buttery-textured soup that's perfect for an elegant first course. For a traditional Dutch accent, accompany the sumptuous soup with dark bread.

to make the soup

Combine the pears, vegetable stock, ginger, and nutmeg in a large saucepan. Bring to a boil over high heat. Reduce the heat; cover and simmer until the pears are very tender, about 10 minutes. Set aside to cool.

to make the salsa

Stir together all the ingredients in a small bowl; set aside.

to complete the recipe

In a separate small saucepan, melt the butter over low heat. Add the flour and stir until smooth, about 1 minute. (Do not let it brown.) Remove from the heat. Gradually whisk in the milk. Place the pan back on medium heat and cook, stirring constantly, until the mixture begins to simmer. Reduce the heat to low and stir constantly until thickened, about 4 minutes. Add the cheese and stir until melted, about 1 minute. Remove from the heat.

Purée the pear mixture in a blender until smooth. Add to the cheese sauce and stir constantly over low heat until heated through. Gradually stir in the apple juice and continue to heat, but do not let the soup come to a boil. Season to taste.

Top each serving with a sprinkling of nutmeg and a mound of salsa.

soup

2	ripe pears, cored, peeled, and coarsely chopped
1½	cups vegetable stock
1	teaspoon minced fresh ginger *(see Tip)*
¼	teaspoon freshly grated nutmeg *(see Tips, page 140)*

salsa

½	unpeeled red-skinned pear, cored and julienned
2	tablespoons fresh lime juice
2	tablespoons minced toasted walnuts *(see Tips, page 35)*
2	tablespoons coarsely chopped dried cranberries *(optional)*
~	dash of freshly grated nutmeg

to complete the recipe

2	tablespoons unsalted butter
2	tablespoons all-purpose flour
1	cup milk
4	ounces baby Gouda cheese, cut into small pieces (about ¾ cup)
½	cup pure apple juice or sweet white wine such as Sauternes
~	salt and ground white pepper to taste
~	freshly grated nutmeg *(see Tips, page 140)* for garnish

Makes 4 cups (4 to 6 servings)

advance preparation

This soup and the salsa are both best when made just before serving.

variation

Substitute aged or smoked Gouda for the baby Gouda.

TIP

Fresh mature ginger should be firm, with a smooth brown skin and no soft spots. To test for freshness, break off one of the knobs; if the ginger is fresh, it will break with a clean snap. Refrigerate in a plastic bag for up to 2 weeks. Peel before using and mince ginger well so the flavor will be distributed evenly in the dish. Ground dried ginger does not have the same distinctive flavor and should not be substituted for fresh in cooked recipes; it can be used in baked goods.

Great food is like great sex—the more you have, the more you want.

—Gael Green

polynesian peanut soup with toasted coconut

Vegan recipe

This distinctive rich and creamy soup was inspired by a favorite peanut sauce. A friend shared the recipe with me over lunch on a South Pacific cruise. Just making it conjures up fond memories of a sunny deck, sensuous breezes, and the bright blue sea.

Toast the coconut in a small dry skillet over medium heat, stirring constantly, until lightly browned, about 5 minutes. Transfer to a plate and set aside to cool.

Heat the oil in a Dutch oven over medium heat. Add the onion, ginger, and garlic; cook, stirring occasionally, until the onion and ginger are very tender, about 10 minutes.

Transfer the onion mixture to a blender. Add the coconut milk, vegetable stock, peanut butter, chutney, and jalapeño; purée until smooth. (It may be necessary to add more vegetable stock if the peanut butter is very thick.)

Transfer the soup to the Dutch oven and stir occasionally over medium heat until heated through. Season to taste.

Meanwhile, toss together the coconut, green onions, and cilantro. Drizzle each serving with sesame oil and top with a mound of the coconut mixture.

1/4	cup sweetened flaked coconut
1	tablespoon canola oil
1	cup finely chopped yellow onion
1/4	cup finely chopped fresh ginger
4	cloves garlic, minced
1	14-ounce can "lite" coconut milk
3/4	cup vegetable stock, or as needed
3/4	cup smooth natural peanut butter *(see Tips)*
1/4	cup mango chutney *(see Tips)*
1	tablespoon minced fresh jalapeño chili, or to taste
~	salt to taste
1/4	cup finely chopped green onions (green parts only)
2	tablespoons minced fresh cilantro
~	Asian sesame oil *(see Tips)* for garnish

Makes 4 cups (4 to 6 servings)

advance preparation

Refrigerate this soup and the toasted coconut in separate covered containers for up to 3 days. When reheating the soup, stir in water to thin as desired.

TIPS

Buy natural peanut butter with oil on the top; stir in the oil before using. Many processed peanut butters are hydrogenated to prevent separation and have sugars, salt, and stabilizers added.

Chutney is a mixture of fruit and/or vegetables, often cooked with vinegar, sugar, and spices. Usually made with mango, chutney is found in most supermarkets; look for it shelved with either the condiments or dressings.

Buy dark, amber-colored Asian sesame oil, made from toasted sesame seeds, rather than light-colored sesame oil, which is extracted from raw sesame seeds and lacks the distinctive strong aroma and nutty flavor. Purchase toasted sesame oil in the Asian section of supermarkets or in Asian markets. After opening, store it in the refrigerator, where it will keep for up to 6 months.

All good cooks learn something new every day.
—Julia Child

french vegetable soup with sherried mushrooms

Vegan recipe if olive oil is substituted for the butter

This full-bodied soup is thickened with cooked winter vegetables, not cream. For an elegant touch, top the soup with sherried mushrooms or a drizzle of truffle oil (see Tips) and garnish with the feathery fennel fronds. Accompany with Gruyère Cheese Crisps (page 162) to add crunch.

to make the soup

Melt the butter in a Dutch oven over medium heat. Add the corn, potatoes, celery, carrot, onion, and fennel. Cook, stirring occasionally, until the vegetables are crisp-tender, about 10 minutes.

Add the vegetable stock, thyme, and bay leaves. Increase the heat to high and bring to a boil. Reduce the heat; cover and simmer until the vegetables are very tender, about 20 minutes.

to prepare the mushrooms

Heat the oil in a medium skillet over medium heat. Add the mushrooms, garlic, and paprika; cook, stirring occasionally, until the mushrooms are tender and lightly browned, about 8 minutes. Reduce the heat to low. Stir in the sherry and lemon juice; stir gently until the liquid is nearly evaporated, about 3 minutes. Remove from the heat and stir in the parsley. Season to taste. Cover to keep warm.

Remove the bay leaves from the soup. In several batches, purée the soup in a blender until smooth.

Return the soup to the pan. Add more vegetable stock if needed.

to complete the recipe

Add the spinach and simmer over medium heat until it is wilted, about 5 minutes. Season to taste.

Top each serving with the mushrooms and a sprig of fennel fronds.

soup

2	tablespoons unsalted butter
2	cups fresh or frozen corn kernels
1	orange-fleshed sweet potato (about 10 ounces), peeled and cut into 3/4-inch chunks (about 2 cups)
1	russet potato (about 10 ounces), peeled and cut into 3/4-inch chunks (about 2 cups)
2	celery stalks with leaves, coarsely chopped
1	carrot, coarsely chopped
1/2	cup coarsely chopped onion
1	fennel bulb, quartered and thinly sliced *(see Tips)*
6	cups vegetable stock, or as needed
2	tablespoons minced fresh thyme, or 1 teaspoon dried thyme
2	bay leaves

mushrooms

2	tablespoons olive oil
2 1/2	cups (6 ounces) sliced cremini mushrooms
2	cloves garlic, minced
3/4	teaspoon sweet paprika, preferably Hungarian
1	tablespoon dry sherry *(see Tip, page 36)*
1	teaspoon fresh lemon juice
1	tablespoon minced fresh flat-leaf parsley
~	salt and freshly ground pepper to taste

Makes 9 cups (8 servings)

advance preparation

This soup will keep for up to 3 days in a covered container in the refrigerator. When reheating, stir in vegetable stock to thin as desired. The mushrooms are best when made just before serving.

variation

Omit the sherried mushrooms; garnish the soup with finely shredded Gruyère cheese and a drizzle of truffle oil (see Tips).

TIPS

Truffles, the highly prized fungi most abundant in France and Italy, have an earthy aroma and rich, subtle flavor with nutty undertones. But fresh truffles are very expensive and hard to find. Truffle oil, available in many gourmet shops, is wonderful drizzled over bread, salads, pasta, or vegetables. Store the oil in the refrigerator for up to 1 year.

Fresh fennel (also called finocchio) looks like a flattened bunch of celery with a large, white, bulbous base and feathery green fronds. To use the bulb, cut off the stalks and discard the bottom end. Cut the bulb in half lengthwise and slice it crosswise into crescent-shaped slices. The stalks are fibrous, with little use other than adding to stocks. The foliage can be used as a garnish or snipped like dill to use for flavoring. Fennel's distinct licorice flavor becomes milder when the vegetable is cooked.

I never eat when I can dine.
—Maurice Chevalier

chunky soups and stews

Chunky soups with lots of vegetables are substantial and satisfying, especially when the vegetables are cut by hand and not a food processor, so the pieces are neat and even, in similar shapes and sizes.

The cooking time of these recipes depends on how soft you like your vegetables. Here, some are simmered in the stock, others roasted in the oven and then added to the soup. Roasting concentrates a vegetable's flavor, while simmering integrates it into the soup. Take care when stirring chunky soups so that the vegetables, especially broccoli florets, don't get broken.

Chunky vegetable soups can be made more robust with the addition of rice, pasta, beans, or nuts, such as Cashew-Carrot Stew (page 107).

Stews are prized for their slow-cooked goodness. My favorite is Pumpkin Stew (page 96), baked in a pumpkin for an easy and spectacular presentation.

Stew served over grains, such as bulgur wheat or couscous, are so chunky you'll want to eat them with a fork. The same holds true for ribollita, minestrone baked with layers of bread, a traditional Tuscan meal made with humble, wholesome ingredients.

These soups benefit from garnishes, which add color and flavor as well as panache.

One cannot think well, love well, sleep well, if one has not dined well.
—Virginia Woolf

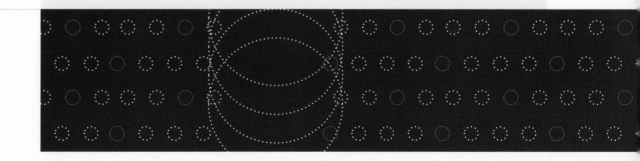

fresh tomato-orange soup with fig quenelles

Vegan recipe if quenelles are omitted.

Sherry and figs balance the fresh, bright flavors of juicy tomatoes and fresh-squeezed orange juice in this surprising soup. Serve it warm or chilled. When tomatoes are not in season, use quality canned or aseptically packaged ones, a better alternative than underripe or flavorless tomatoes.

to make the quenelles

Put the figs in a small saucepan and add water to cover. Bring to a boil over medium heat. Reduce the heat; cover and simmer until softened, about 10 minutes. Drain the figs and coarsely chop. Purée in a food processor with the remaining ingredients. Form into 4 or 6 ovals by pressing the mixture into a tablespoon with your fingers. Set aside.

to make the soup

Put the chopped tomatoes in a sieve set over a bowl; set aside to drain. Reserve the juice.

Heat the oil in a Dutch oven over medium heat. Add the onion; cook, stirring occasionally, until translucent, about 5 minutes. Add the tomatoes and garlic; cook, stirring occasionally, until tender, about 5 minutes.

Add vegetable stock to the tomato juice so the liquid equals 1 1/2 cups; pour into the pan and add the red pepper flakes (if using). Tie the thyme and basil together with kitchen twine; immerse in the soup. Increase the heat to high and bring to a boil. Reduce the heat; cover and simmer until the onion is very tender, about 15 minutes.

Remove the herbs and discard. Stir in the orange juice, brown sugar, pepper, and salt. Taste and adjust the seasoning.

Divide the soup among 4 or 6 shallow bowls. Place 1 quenelle in each serving.

quenelles

4 dried figs, stemmed

1 teaspoon cream sherry *(see Tip, page 36)*

1/4 cup crème fraîche *(see Tip, page 147)*

1/4 teaspoon sugar

soup

6 large ripe tomatoes (about 3 pounds), peeled and coarsely chopped *(see Tips)*

2 tablespoons olive oil

1 cup finely chopped onion

2 cloves garlic, minced

1 1/2 cups vegetable stock, or as needed

~ pinch of red pepper flakes *(optional)*

1 sprig fresh thyme

1 sprig fresh basil

1/2 cup fresh orange juice

1 tablespoon packed light brown sugar, or to taste

1/4 teaspoon freshly ground pepper, or to taste

~ salt to taste

Makes 5 cups (4 to 6 servings)

advance preparation

This soup will keep for up to 3 days in a covered container in the refrigerator. Serve chilled or reheat. Refrigerate the quenelles in a covered container for up to 3 days; bring to room temperature before serving.

variation

Substitute one 28-ounce can tomatoes for the fresh tomatoes. Drain the tomatoes, reserving the juice; combine the juice with vegetable stock as needed to equal 1 1/2 cups liquid.

TIPS

Store unwashed tomatoes, stem-end down, at room temperature. Do not refrigerate; temperatures below 55° F make tomatoes spongy and destroy their flavor.

To peel a tomato, first core it with a paring knife, removing the stem end and white center. Cut an X on the bottom of the tomato, carefully piercing just through the skin. Using a slotted spoon, plunge the tomato into boiling water just long enough to loosen the skin without cooking the tomato (about 5 seconds for a very ripe tomato, or 10 to 20 seconds for a firmer tomato). Remove the tomato with the slotted spoon and immediately plunge it into a bowl of ice water; let stand for about 1 minute. This will stop the tomato from cooking and further loosen the skin. Drain and let cool to the touch. Use a paring knife to peel away the skin.

Eating well gives a spectacular joy to life.
—Elsa Schiaparelli

black bean soup with mango salsa

Vegan recipe

Sweet and juicy mango is an unexpected, colorful, and refreshing complement to the bold, spicy flavors of chunky bean soup.

to make the salsa

Combine the lime juice and brown sugar in a medium bowl, whisking until the sugar is dissolved. Gently stir in all the remaining salsa ingredients. Set aside at room temperature to allow the flavors to blend.

to make the soup

Heat the oil in a Dutch oven over medium heat. Add the onion, carrot, celery, and garlic; cook, stirring occasionally, until the vegetables are crisp-tender, about 8 minutes. Add the cumin and coriander; stir for about 30 seconds.

Stir in all the remaining ingredients, except the salt. Increase the heat to high and bring to a boil. Reduce the heat; cover and simmer until the vegetables are tender, about 20 minutes.

Transfer 1 cup of the beans and liquid to a blender and purée until smooth. Stir the puréed mixture into the soup. Taste and adjust the seasoning.

Serve in shallow bowls (to prevent the salsa from sinking to the bottom of the bowl) and top each serving with a mound of the salsa.

salsa

2	tablespoons fresh lime juice
1	teaspoon packed light brown sugar
1	ripe mango, cut into $3/8$-inch dice *(see Tip)*
2	tablespoons minced red onion
2	tablespoons minced fresh cilantro
1	teaspoon minced fresh jalapeño chili, or to taste
~	salt to taste

soup

2	tablespoons olive oil
1	cup finely chopped onion
1	carrot, finely chopped
1	celery stalk, finely chopped
4	cloves garlic, minced
1/2	teaspoon ground cumin
1/2	teaspoon ground coriander
3	cups vegetable stock
1/2	cup fresh orange juice
1	15-ounce can black beans, drained and rinsed
1/4	teaspoon freshly ground pepper, or to taste
1/8	teaspoon red pepper flakes, or to taste
~	salt to taste

Makes 4 cups (4 servings)

This soup will keep for up to 5 days in a covered container in the refrigerator. Refrigerate the salsa in a covered container for up to 2 days; bring to room temperature before serving.

TIP

Mangos are usually sold quite firm; ripen, uncovered, at room temperature, turning occasionally. Refrigerate ripe fruit in a plastic or paper bag for up to 3 days.

A ripe mango is difficult to cut neatly because the pulpy flesh is very juicy and clings to the flat pit. The simplest method is to stand the mango upright on a cutting board and slice slightly off center through the flesh on one of the flatter sides, curving around the seed. Repeat on the other side to make 2 disklike portions, plus a center section with the seed. Place one mango half, skin-side down, on a cutting board or in the palm of one hand. Score the flesh all the way to the skin in a checkerboard pattern, cutting to but not through the outer skin. Carefully push up the skin side to expose cubes of flesh. Then cut the mango cubes from the peel. For the center section, slice off the skin, then cut the flesh away from the seed or enjoy the juicy, sweet center over the sink.

When I have eaten mangoes, I have felt like Eve.
—Rose Macaulay

red lentil soup with pita croutons

Vegan recipe, depending on ingredients in pitas (check package label)

This fragrant recipe was inspired by *shorbet adds,* an Egyptian soup that is sold by street vendors in Cairo. Served with fried onions and pita croutons, it's a great main course. Red lentils do not retain their lovely salmon color when cooked, but they're still delicious. Take care not to overcook them; they should be tender but not mushy.

to make the soup

Heat the oil in a Dutch oven over medium heat. Add the onions and garlic; cook, stirring occasionally, until the onions are translucent, about 5 minutes. Add the cumin and coriander; stir for about 30 seconds.

Stir in 6 cups of the vegetable stock, the lentils, carrots, celery leaves, and red pepper flakes. Increase the heat to high and bring to a boil. Reduce the heat; cover and simmer, stirring occasionally, until the lentils are tender, about 30 minutes. Stir in the remaining 2 cups of stock and the lemon juice. Season to taste.

to prepare the garnishes

Adjust the oven rack to 4 to 5 inches from the broiler heating element; preheat the broiler. Heat the oil in a large skillet over medium-low heat. Add the onion and cook, stirring occasionally, until very tender and lightly browned, about 10 minutes.

Place the pita halves on a baking sheet; toast under the broiler until crispy and light brown, about 2 minutes per side. Let cool, then break into 1-inch pieces.

Top each serving with a mound of the cooked onion and sprinkle with the pita croutons; serve a lemon wedge on the side.

soup

2 tablespoons olive oil

2 cups finely chopped onions

3 cloves garlic, minced

1 teaspoon ground cumin

1 teaspoon ground coriander

8 cups vegetable stock

1¾ cups dried red lentils
(see Tip, page 91)

2 carrots, finely chopped

½ cup coarsely chopped celery leaves

~ pinch of red pepper flakes

¼ cup fresh lemon juice

~ salt and freshly ground pepper to taste

garnishes

2 tablespoons olive oil

1 large onion, thinly sliced

2 pita pocket breads, halved horizontally *(see Tip)*

6–8 lemon wedges

Makes 7 cups (6 to 8 servings)

advance preparation

This soup will keep for up to 5 days in a covered container in the refrigerator. When reheating, stir in vegetable stock or water to thin as desired. Store the pita croutons for up to 5 days in a tightly covered tin at room temperature.

variation

Substitute brown lentils for the red lentils; increase the cooking time to about 35 minutes, or until the lentils are tender.

TIP

Mediterranean or Greek pitas are sometimes called pita pocket breads; the breads can be cut to form 2 pockets or can be split horizontally to make 2 thin rounds. Lebanese pita bread has no pocket and cannot be split horizontally; it is served as a flat bread. Check package labeling to be certain you select the appropriate bread to suit your use.

Lentils without onions are like a dance without music.
—Greek proverb

arborio rice soup

Vegan recipe if cheese garnish is omitted

Arborio rice is an Italian short-grain, high-starch rice used in risotto, Spanish paella, and rice puddings because the grains impart a creamy texture. Use any orange-fleshed winter squash in this soup; they are all sweet and creamy when cooked.

Heat the oil in a Dutch oven over medium heat. Add the onion, celery and leaves, and garlic; cook, stirring occasionally, until the onion is translucent, about 5 minutes. Add the mushrooms; continue to cook, stirring occasionally, until the mushrooms are tender, about 5 minutes.

Add the rice and rosemary; stir until coated with oil. Add the vegetable stock, squash, and lemon zest strips. Increase the heat to high and bring to a boil. Reduce the heat; cover and simmer, stirring occasionally, until the rice and squash are tender, about 12 minutes.

Stir in the lemon juice and season to taste. Serve topped with cheese.

62

1	tablespoon olive oil
1	cup finely chopped onion
1	celery stalk with leaves, finely chopped
3	cloves garlic, minced
2½	cups (6 ounces) sliced cremini mushrooms *(see Tips)*
½	cup Arborio rice *(see Tips)*
1	teaspoon minced fresh rosemary, or ½ teaspoon dried rosemary, crushed *(see Tips, page 115)*
4	cups vegetable stock
1	16-ounce acorn squash, peeled, seeded, and cut into ½-inch dice (about 2 cups)
1	teaspoon thin strips lemon zest *(see Tips, page 131)*
2	tablespoons fresh lemon juice
~	salt and freshly ground pepper to taste
~	very thin slices of pecorino Romano cheese *(see Tips)* for garnish

Makes 5 cups (4 servings)

advance preparation

This soup will keep for up to 3 days in a covered container in the refrigerator. When reheating, stir in vegetable stock or water to thin as desired.

variations

~ Substitute dry white wine for $1/2$ cup of the vegetable stock.

~ Omit the squash when cooking the soup; serve the soup in Roasted Acorn Squash Soup Bowls (page 152).

TIPS

Cremini mushrooms (sometimes labeled "Italian brown mushrooms") are more flavorful and have a denser, less watery texture than ordinary white mushrooms. Portobello mushrooms are larger, matured cremini.

Mushrooms are like sponges and will absorb water. Some pros advise cleaning them with a paper towel or soft brush. Others recommend a quick rinse just before using. Don't store mushrooms in plastic (it traps moisture), but in paper bags or between paper towels in the refrigerator. Also, keep them away from strong-flavored foods because they will pick up odors.

It's important not to rinse Arborio rice before cooking. Rinsing will wash away the starch necessary to create the creamy texture.

Taking their name from the city of Rome, there are several different styles of Romano cheese. The best known is the sharp, tangy imported pecorino Romano, which is made with sheep's milk. Most domestic Romanos are made of cow's milk, or a combination of cow's milk and goat's or sheep's milk. The cheeses are very firm and used most often for grating.

moroccan chickpea soup with roasted red pepper coulis

Vegan recipe

Inspired by hummus, the flavor-packed Middle Eastern spread, this soup is best served with traditional wedges of fresh Lebanese pita bread (see Tip, page 61) or Toasted Pita Triangles, the crispy version on page 159.

to make the coulis

>**Combine** all the ingredients in a food processor or blender and process, pushing down the sides occasionally, until smooth and creamy; set aside to allow the flavors to blend.

to make the soup

>**Heat the oil** in a Dutch oven over medium heat. Add the carrots, onion, bell pepper, and garlic; cook, stirring occasionally, until crisp-tender, about 6 minutes. Add the cumin; stir for about 30 seconds.
>
>**Meanwhile,** purée the chickpeas, 1 cup of the vegetable stock, and the lemon juice in a blender until smooth.
>
>**Stir the puréed mixture** into the soup, then add the remaining 2 cups stock and all the other ingredients, except the minced parsley and garnishes. Increase the heat to high and bring to a boil. Reduce the heat; cover and simmer until the carrots are tender, about 10 minutes. Stir in the minced parsley. Taste and adjust the seasoning.
>
>**Top each serving** with a swirl of the coulis, a sprinkling of cracked pepper, and a sprig of parsley.

coulis

1/4	cup coarsely chopped jarred roasted red bell pepper
1	teaspoon extra-virgin olive oil
1	teaspoon red wine vinegar
1/4	teaspoon sugar
~	salt and freshly ground pepper to taste

soup

2	tablespoons olive oil
2	carrots, cut into 1/4-inch dice
3/4	cup finely chopped onion
1/2	cup finely chopped red bell pepper
2	cloves garlic, minced
3/4	teaspoon ground cumin
1	15-ounce can chickpeas (garbanzo beans), drained and rinsed *(see Tips)*
3	cups vegetable stock
2	tablespoons fresh lemon juice
2	teaspoons minced fresh thyme, or 1/2 teaspoon dried thyme
1/2	teaspoon freshly ground pepper, or to taste
1/4	teaspoon ground turmeric
1/8	teaspoon cayenne pepper, or to taste

Makes 4 cups (4 servings)

64

~ salt to taste

1 tablespoon minced fresh
flat-leaf parsley, plus fresh
flat-leaf parsley sprigs for
garnish

~ coarsely cracked black
pepper *(see Tips)*

advance preparation

Refrigerate this soup and the coulis in separate covered containers for up to 5 days. When reheating the soup, stir in vegetable stock to thin as desired. Bring the coulis to room temperature before serving.

TIPS

Chickpeas are often sold canned as garbanzo beans, and they are sometimes called ceci beans.

Freshly ground or cracked whole dried peppercorns are more flavorful than preground pepper because, once cracked, the peppercorn immediately releases much of its oil, thus losing aroma and taste. The best pepper grinders have settings for both coarse and fine grinds. For extra-coarse chunks of pepper, crack the peppercorns by pressing them firmly on a cutting board with the side of a chef's knife. Always buy the largest peppercorns available because their longer growing time gives them a fuller flavor.

farina dumpling soup

Vegan recipe if dumplings are omitted and soup is made with pasta

These light and tender dumplings have become a family favorite ever since my friend Marie Wintergerst shared the recipe that nourished her children and is still requested when they return home as adults.

to make the dumplings

Stir together the egg, Cream of Wheat, and vegetable oil in a small bowl. Cover and refrigerate for 20 minutes. To cook, bring a medium saucepan of salted vegetable stock to a boil over high heat. Drop the batter by scant teaspoonfuls (the dumplings will be irregular in shape) into the stock. Reduce the heat; simmer for about 20 minutes, or until the dumplings expand and are cooked through. When they are done, use a slotted spoon to transfer the dumplings to a plate; cover to keep warm. Discard the stock.

to make the soup

Heat the oil in a Dutch oven over medium heat. Add the carrots and onion; cook, stirring occasionally, until the carrots are crisp-tender, about 5 minutes.
Add the vegetable stock. Increase the heat to high and bring to a boil. Stir in all the remaining ingredients. Reduce the heat; cover and simmer until the vegetables are tender, about 10 minutes.
Remove the bay leaf and season to taste.
For each serving, place 2 or 3 dumplings in a soup bowl and ladle the hot soup over them.

dumplings
- **1** egg, lightly beaten
- **1/4** cup regular (not instant) Cream of Wheat
- **2** teaspoons vegetable oil
- **6** cups vegetable stock, or as needed
- **~** salt to taste

soup
- **1** tablespoon olive oil
- **2** carrots, cut into 1/4-inch slices
- **1/2** cup coarsely chopped onion
- **6** cups vegetable stock
- **2** celery stalks with leaves, thinly sliced
- **2** plum tomatoes, cut into 1/2-inch chunks
- **2** tablespoons minced fresh flat-leaf parsley
- **2** tablespoons minced fresh thyme, or 1 teaspoon dried thyme
- **2** teaspoons snipped fresh dill, or 1/2 teaspoon dried dill *(see Tips)*
- **1** bay leaf *(see Tips)*
- **~** salt and freshly ground pepper to taste

Makes 6 cups with 12 dumplings
(4 to 6 servings)

advance preparation

This soup and the dumplings will keep for up to 3 days in separate covered containers in the refrigerator. It's easiest to assemble individual servings of the soup with dumplings and reheat in the microwave. Or, reheat them together in a Dutch oven for no longer than 10 minutes, taking care not to break the dumplings apart.

variations

~ Omit the dumplings; with the vegetables, add 3/4 cup rosamarina, orzo, or riso pasta (tiny rice-shaped pastas) or 2 cups wide egg noodles. Cook in the vegetable stock, adjusting the timing according to the pasta package instructions.

~ Omit the dumplings; with the vegetables, add 6 to 8 ounces mushroom- or cheese-filled tortellini. Cook, adjusting the timing according to the tortellini package instructions.

TIPS

Dill is a sharply aromatic herb with a mild, lemony taste. When using fresh dill, cut the feathery dill tips with scissors. Dried dill is acceptable, but it is stronger than fresh, so use it in moderation.

Bay leaf is an aromatic herb that comes from the evergreen bay laurel tree, native to the Mediterranean. Fresh leaves are seldom available, but dried bay leaves can be found in the herb section of most supermarkets. Store them in an airtight container in a cool, dark place for up to 6 months. Since overuse will make a dish bitter, use them in moderation to flavor soups and stews, and be sure to remove before serving.

wild rice-cranberry soup

Wild rice, which is actually an aquatic grainlike seed rather than a rice, grows in marshy bogs, lakes, and rivers. Wild rice is a favorite in Minnesota, where I live, especially around the holidays, when it is appreciated for its nutty flavor. In this soup it is paired with tart-sweet cranberries and sherry to add elegance.

Melt the butter in a Dutch oven over medium heat. Add the carrot, celery, and onion; cook, stirring occasionally, until the carrot is tender, about 8 minutes.

Add the flour and stir until smooth. Gradually add the vegetable stock, whisking constantly to prevent lumps. Increase the heat to medium-high and stir until the soup is thickened, about 5 minutes. Stir in the rice and cranberries. Reduce the heat; cover and simmer, stirring occasionally, until the cranberries are softened and plumped, about 15 minutes.

Stir in all the remaining ingredients, except the garnishes. Stir occasionally until warmed through. Season to taste.

Sprinkle each serving with pepper and sage.

advance preparation

This soup will keep for up to 3 days in a covered container in the refrigerator. When reheating, stir in milk to thin as desired.

TIP

To cook wild rice, first rinse it in a strainer under cold running water or in a bowl of water; drain. Bring 2 cups water, 1/2 cup rice, and 1/2 teaspoon salt to a boil in a heavy saucepan over medium-high heat. Reduce the heat; cover and simmer until the rice kernels are opened and slightly chewy rather than mushy, 45 to 55 minutes; drain well. Makes about 1 1/2 cups.

4	tablespoons unsalted butter
1	carrot, finely chopped
1	celery stalk, finely chopped
1/2	cup finely chopped onion
3	tablespoons all-purpose flour
3	cups vegetable stock
1 1/2	cups cooked wild rice *(see Tip)*
1/2	cup dried cranberries
1	cup milk or half-and-half
2	tablespoons dry sherry *(optional; see Tip, page 36)*
~	salt and freshly ground pepper to taste
~	Fried Sage *(page 163)* or minced fresh flat-leaf parsley for garnish

Makes 5 cups (4 to 6 servings)

asparagus-leek soup

This luxurious soup is one of my favorite first courses. To trim asparagus, hold a stalk and snap it at the point where it naturally gives easily. This eliminates the woody, tough end, while keeping the tender top, the best part.

Steam the asparagus in a covered steamer over boiling water until crisp-tender. Or, put the asparagus in a microwave-proof dish and add about 1/4 cup water. Cover tightly and microwave on high for about 4 minutes. Drain well; set aside.

Melt 1 tablespoon of the butter in a small skillet over medium heat. Add the corn and bell pepper; cook, stirring occasionally, until tender, about 5 minutes. **Add salt** to taste. Set aside.

Melt the remaining 3 tablespoons butter in a Dutch oven over medium heat. Add the mushrooms and leeks; cook, stirring occasionally, until tender but not brown, about 5 minutes. Add the curry powder; stir for about 30 seconds. Add the vegetable stock, milk, and asparagus. Increase the heat to medium-high and stir occasionally as the liquid comes to a simmer, then reduce the heat to medium.

Stir together the cornstarch and cold water in a small bowl until smooth; stir into the soup. Cook, stirring constantly, until the soup is smooth and slightly thickened, about 2 minutes. Remove from the heat. Season to taste.

Top each serving with about 2 tablespoons of the corn mixture.

1 pound asparagus spears, trimmed and cut into 1 1/2-inch lengths (about 4 cups)

4 tablespoons unsalted butter

1 1/2 cups fresh or frozen corn kernels

1/3 cup finely chopped red bell pepper

~ salt to taste

2 1/2 cups (6 ounces) sliced cremini mushrooms

3 leeks (white parts only), halved lengthwise, rinsed, and cut into 1/8-inch slices *(see Tips)*

1/2 teaspoon curry powder

2 cups vegetable stock

2 cups milk

4 teaspoons cornstarch

3 tablespoons cold water

~ salt and ground white pepper to taste *(see Tips)*

Makes 5 cups (4 to 6 servings)

advance preparation

This soup is best the day it is prepared, but it will keep for up to 3 days in a covered container in the refrigerator. When reheating, stir in vegetable stock or milk to thin as desired.

TIPS

Leeks look like overgrown green onions and have a mild onion-and-garlic flavor. Select those with crisp, bright green leaves and unblemished white bulbs. Buy the smallest in the market; leeks under 1$\frac{1}{2}$ inches in diameter are the sweetest and most tender. Refrigerate them in a perforated plastic bag for up to 1 week. Before using, trim the rootlets, tough green tops, and coarse outer leaves; use the white base and up to 1 inch of the pale green part attached to the white. To remove the grit and sand trapped between the many layers, cut the leek lengthwise and slice or chop; swish the pieces around in a bowl of warm water. When the dirt settles to the bottom of the bowl, lift out the clean pieces.

Peppercorns are berries that grow in grapelike clusters on a climbing vine. Black peppercorns are picked when the berries are not quite ripe; when dried, they turn from dark brown to black. White peppercorns have been allowed to ripen, after which the skin is removed and the berries are dried. They are smaller, smoother skinned, and have a milder flavor than black peppercorns. White pepper is often used in light-colored foods where the specks of black pepper would stand out. Whole dried peppercorns can be stored in a cool, dark place for about 1 year; ground pepper remains flavorful for about 4 months.

ratatouille soup

Vegan recipe if cheese garnish is omitted

This thick and chunky ratatouille soup is hearty and satisfying. Serve it hot or chilled, accompanied with thick slices of crusty French bread, wedges of pita bread, or Toasted Pita Triangles (page 159).

Heat the oil in a Dutch oven over medium heat. Add the onion; cook, stirring occasionally, until it is translucent, about 8 minutes. Stir in the eggplant, zucchini, green beans, bell pepper, and garlic. Sprinkle the vinegar over the vegetables. Cover and cook, stirring occasionally, for about 10 minutes.

Stir in the tomato sauce, oregano, dried basil (if using), sugar, and pepper. Increase the heat to high and bring to a boil. Reduce the heat; cover and simmer, stirring occasionally, over low heat until the vegetables are tender, about 30 minutes.

Stir in the vegetable stock, tomatoes, and fresh basil (if using), and salt. Increase the heat to medium; cover and cook, stirring occasionally, for about 5 minutes, or until the tomatoes are tender. Taste and adjust the seasoning.

Garnish each serving with cheese.

Eat some, leave some;
remember tomorrow.
—Jamaican proverb

2	tablespoons olive oil
1	onion, cut into 1/4-inch strips (about 1 cup)
1	eggplant (about 12 ounces), peeled and cut into 2-by-1/4-inch strips *(see Tip)*
1	zucchini, cut into 2-by-1/4-inch strips (about 1 cup)
1	cup chopped green beans in 2-inch lengths (about 4 ounces)
1/2	green bell pepper, seeded, deribbed, and cut into 2-by-1/4-inch strips
2	cloves garlic, minced
2	tablespoons red wine vinegar
1	15-ounce can tomato sauce
1	tablespoon minced fresh oregano, or 1 teaspoon dried oregano
1	tablespoon minced fresh basil, or 1 teaspoon dried basil
1	teaspoon sugar, or to taste
1/2	teaspoon freshly ground pepper, or to taste
1	cup vegetable stock
2	tomatoes, peeled and cut into 1/2-inch dice *(see Tips, page 57)*
~	salt to taste
~	shredded Cheddar, Monterey Jack, or Parmesan cheese for garnish

Makes 6 cups (4 to 6 servings)

72

This soup will keep for up to 5 days in a covered container in the refrigerator. When reheating, stir in vegetable stock, water, or tomato juice to thin as desired.

TIP

Eggplants, which are actually a fruit, not a vegetable, are available in many varieties; the most common is pear-shaped with a smooth, glossy dark purple skin. Under the skin, most varieties are pretty much alike and are interchangeable in recipes. Because eggplants become bitter with age, it's best to select smaller, young fruits, which do not require salting and rinsing before using. Press gently on the flesh; if the eggplant is ripe, it will spring right back. If a dent remains, it is past its prime. Store eggplant in a plastic bag in the vegetable drawer of the refrigerator and use within a day or two of purchase. Since the flesh discolors rapidly, cut the eggplant just before using.

73

jalapeño-corn chowder

Although we think of corn as a Midwestern summer vegetable, it's actually grown year-round in Florida, the number-one sweet corn–producing state. (California is second.) Nothing beats corn eaten the same day that it's picked, in its prime, before the sugar begins to turn to starch. But when garden-fresh corn is unavailable, frozen corn will do.

Melt the butter in a Dutch oven over medium-low heat. Add the onion, carrot, bell pepper, celery and leaves, and garlic; cook, stirring occasionally, until tender, about 10 minutes.

Stir in the vegetable stock, corn, potato, and jalapeño. Increase the heat to high and bring to a boil. Reduce the heat; cover and simmer until the potato is tender, about 10 minutes.

Remove the jalapeño chili and discard. Transfer 2 cups of the soup mixture to a blender and purée with the milk. Return the puréed mixture to the soup.

Heat, stirring occasionally, until warmed through. Season to taste. Garnish each serving with a sprinkling of chili sauce and a small mound of cheese.

2	tablespoons unsalted butter
1	cup coarsely chopped onion
1	carrot, coarsely shredded
1/2	red bell pepper, seeded, deribbed, and finely chopped
1	celery stalk with leaves, finely chopped
2	cloves garlic, minced
3	cups vegetable stock
2	cups fresh or frozen corn kernels
1	large russet potato (about 12 ounces), peeled and cut into 3/4-inch dice (about 2 1/4 cups)
1/2	fresh jalapeño chili, cut in half lengthwise and seeded (see Tips)
1	cup milk
~	salt and freshly ground pepper to taste
~	dash of hot chili sauce and finely shredded Cheddar cheese for garnish

advance preparation

This soup will keep for up to 3 days in a covered container in the refrigerator. When reheating, stir in vegetable stock or milk to thin as desired.

TIP

A chilie's heat depends on its capsaicin content, found in its veins inside the flesh. Unaffected by heat or cold, capsaicin retains its potency through cooking or freezing. Removing the ribs and seeds before using chilies is a way to reduce the heat. Or, you can soak them in heavily salted water for several hours. Small chilies have more membranes and seeds than large ones, so generally they are hotter.

To avoid irritation from the caustic oils in chilies, do not touch your eyes, nose, or lips while handling them. Many cooks wear disposable plastic gloves when working with hot chilies. Afterward, wash your hands, knife, and cutting board in hot, soapy water.

People have tried and they have tried, but
sex is not better than sweet corn.
—Garrison Keillor

tortilla soup with avocado-corn salsa

Vegan recipe, depending on ingredients in tortillas (check package label)

Salsa and chips in a bowl. This is a soup for kids who want to eat their favorite snack for dinner. When it's available, I like to make the salsa using white shoe-peg corn (see Tip) because I like its sweet flavor.

to make the salsa

Whisk together the oil, lime juice, jalapeño, garlic, and sugar in a small bowl. Gently stir in the avocado, corn, red onion, and cilantro. Season to taste; set aside.

to make the soup

Heat the oil in a Dutch oven over medium heat. Add the onion, bell pepper, celery and leaves, and garlic; cook, stirring occasionally, until the vegetables are crisp-tender, about 8 minutes. Add the cumin; stir for about 30 seconds.

Stir in the vegetable stock, tomatoes, beans, pepper, and red pepper flakes. Increase the heat to high and bring to a boil. Reduce the heat; cover and simmer until the vegetables are tender, about 20 minutes. Stir in the parsley and salt. Taste and adjust the seasoning.

to prepare the tortilla strips

Heat the olive oil in a large skillet over medium heat. Add the tortilla strips in a single layer. Cook, turning occasionally with tongs, until the strips are lightly browned and crispy, about 10 minutes. Transfer the strips to a plate lined with a paper towel.

Top each bowl of soup with tortilla strips and a mound of the salsa.

---

salsa

1	tablespoon extra-virgin olive oil
1	tablespoon fresh lime juice
2	teaspoons minced fresh jalapeño chili, or to taste
2	cloves garlic, minced
1/4	teaspoon sugar
1	avocado, peeled, pitted, and cut into 1/2-inch dice
1/4	cup frozen corn kernels, thawed
2	tablespoons minced red onion
2	tablespoons minced fresh cilantro, or to taste
~	salt and freshly ground pepper to taste

soup

1	tablespoon olive oil
1	cup coarsely chopped onion
1/2	red bell pepper, seeded, deribbed, and coarsely chopped
1	celery stalk with leaves, coarsely chopped
4	cloves garlic, minced
1/2	teaspoon ground cumin
3	cups vegetable stock
1	15-ounce can stewed tomatoes
1	15-ounce can garbanzo beans or black beans, drained and rinsed

This soup will keep for up to 5 days in a covered container in the refrigerator. Prepare the salsa and tortilla strips the day of serving. Refrigerate the salsa in a covered container; store the strips in a tightly covered tin at room temperature.

TIP

White shoepeg corn kernels, named for their peglike shape, are available frozen. The kernels are smaller and sweeter than regular yellow corn kernels.

1/2 teaspoon freshly ground pepper, or to taste

~ pinch of red pepper flakes, or to taste

2 tablespoons minced fresh flat-leaf parsley

~ salt to taste

tortilla strips

2 tablespoons olive oil

3 6-inch corn tortillas, halved and cut into 1/4-inch strips

caramelized onion soup with herbed goat cheese toasts

Vegan recipe if onions are cooked in olive oil not butter and if goat cheese toast is omitted.

The secret to a good onion soup is cooking the onions slowly long enough for the flavors to develop and their sugars to caramelize. Serve this soup in ovenproof bowls, so the goat cheese (which I prefer over the traditional, hearty Gruyère) can soften under the broiler.

to make the soup

Melt the butter in a Dutch oven over medium heat. Add the onions and stir well to coat with the butter. Reduce the heat to medium–low; cover and cook, stirring occasionally, until the onions are very tender, about 25 minutes. Increase the heat to medium; uncover and continue to cook, stirring frequently, until the onions are lightly browned, about 15 minutes. (Don't let the onions burn, or they'll become bitter.)

Add the shallots and garlic; cook, stirring constantly, for about 2 minutes. Add the wine and increase the heat to medium–high; cook, stirring constantly, until the liquid is completely evaporated, about 3 minutes. Add the vegetable stock and thyme; bring to a boil. Reduce the heat; cover and simmer, stirring occasionally, for about 20 minutes. Season to taste.

to prepare the toasts

Position an oven rack about 4 to 5 inches from the broiler heating element; preheat the broiler. Stir together the goat cheese, olive oil, garlic, rosemary, salt, and pepper in a small bowl. Arrange the bread slices in a single layer on a baking sheet. Lightly toast under the broiler for about 1 minute on each side, or until crusty on the outside, soft on the inside. Spread each bread slice with the goat cheese mixture.

continued . . .

soup

4	tablespoons unsalted butter
1	pound Vidalias or other sweet onions, thinly sliced (about 6 cups; *see Tips, page 80*)
1/2	pound red onions, thinly sliced (about 3 cups)
1/2	cup thinly sliced shallots
4	cloves garlic, minced
2/3	cup dry red wine
3	cups vegetable stock
1	tablespoon minced fresh thyme, or 1 teaspoon dried thyme
~	salt and freshly ground pepper to taste

toasts

1/4	cup (2 ounces) fresh white goat cheese (*chèvre; see Tips, page 80*)
1	teaspoon extra-virgin olive oil
1	small garlic clove, minced
1/2	teaspoon minced fresh rosemary, or a pinch of dried rosemary, crushed (*see Tip, page 10*)
~	dash of salt and freshly ground pepper
8	1/2-inch slices baguette

Makes 4 cups (4 servings)

Reposition the oven rack to about 6 inches from the broiler heating element. To serve, pour the soup into ovenproof bowls placed on a baking sheet. Float 2 toasts in a single layer in each bowl and place under the broiler for about 1 minute, or until the cheese is softened. Serve immediately.

advance preparation

This soup will keep for up to 2 days in a covered container in the refrigerator. The bread can be toasted early in the day; store on a lightly covered plate at room temperature. Spread the toasts with goat cheese and broil atop the soup just before serving.

TIPS

Sweet onions are thin-skinned and somewhat flat in shape, including Vidalias from Georgia, Spring Sweets from Texas, Walla Wallas from Washington, Mauis from Hawaii, and OSO Sweets from Chile. These onions contain more water than regular onions, so they do not keep as long. They're also lower in the sulfur compounds that give most onions their characteristic bite and their power to cause tears. Store all onions in a cool, dry place with good ventilation. Keep them away from potatoes, which give off moisture that causes onions to rot.

Goat cheese (*chèvre* in French) is made from goat's milk and may be either fresh and white or coated with herbs and pepper, and is aged to varying degrees. Domestic goat cheese is a fine substitute for the more expensive imported brands. Once opened, tightly wrap fresh goat cheese in plastic and store it in the refrigerator for up to 2 weeks, or marinate it in olive oil for longer storage. (Do not confuse fresh white goat cheese with feta cheese or caprini, Italian goat cheese, which is aged, less creamy, and more acidic.)

Life is like an onion. You peel off one layer
at a time; and sometimes you weep.
—Carl Sandburg

cashew chili

Vegan recipe if cheese garnish is omitted

In my home, this chili is a fall tradition, and I serve it with a green salad tossed with a creamy dressing and warm corn muffins. Leftover chili, if there is any, is delicious over split baked potatoes. Pop them under the broiler to melt a topping of cheese.

Heat the oil in an a Dutch oven over medium heat. Add the onion, bell pepper, celery, and garlic; cook, stirring occasionally, until the vegetables are crisp-tender, about 8 minutes.

Stir in the tomatoes with juice, beans, tomato sauce, water, corn, chili powder, Tabasco sauce, cumin, oregano, and dried basil (if using), bay leaf, and pepper. Increase the heat to high and bring to a boil. Reduce the heat; cover and simmer, stirring occasionally, for 15 minutes.

Stir in the cashews and raisins; continue to simmer, covered, until the raisins are plump and the cashews are tender, about 20 minutes. During the last 5 minutes, stir in the fresh basil (if using). Remove the bay leaf. Taste and adjust the seasoning.

Top each serving with cheese.

advance preparation

If possible, prepare this chili 1 day in advance to allow the flavors to blend; refrigerate in a covered container for up to 5 days. When reheating, stir in water, vegetable stock, or tomato juice to thin as desired.

TIP

Once opened, refrigerate Tabasco (hot pepper) sauce to retain its zesty flavor and red color.

2	tablespoons olive oil
1	cup coarsely chopped onion
1	green bell pepper, seeded, deribbed, and coarsely chopped
2	celery stalks, coarsely chopped
2	cloves garlic, minced
1	28-ounce can tomatoes with juice, tomatoes halved
1	15-ounce can kidney beans, drained and rinsed
1	15-ounce can tomato sauce
1	cup water
1	cup fresh or frozen corn kernels
2	teaspoons chili powder, or to taste
1/2	teaspoon Tabasco sauce, or to taste *(see Tip)*
1	teaspoon ground cumin
1	tablespoon minced fresh oregano, or 1 teaspoon dried oregano
1	tablespoon minced fresh basil, or 1 teaspoon dried basil
1	bay leaf
1/2	teaspoon freshly ground pepper, or to taste
1	cup whole raw cashews
1	cup dark raisins
~	salt to taste
~	shredded Monterey Jack or Cheddar cheese for garnish

Makes 8 cups (6 to 8 servings)

broccoli-cheese soup with caraway bread crumbs

Caraway bread crumbs give this hearty soup a fine edge. Serve with a green salad, crusty rolls, and a crisp dry Riesling wine or German beer for a fine fall meal.

to make the bread crumbs

Melt the butter in a small skillet over low heat. Add the bread crumbs and stir constantly until lightly browned, about 2 minutes. Transfer to a bowl and set aside to cool. Toss in the parsley. Set aside.

to make the soup

Melt the butter in a Dutch oven over medium heat. Add the carrot, onion, bell pepper, and garlic; cook, stirring occasionally, until the vegetables are tender, about 10 minutes. Add the flour; stir constantly over low heat for about 2 minutes. Gradually add the vegetable stock, whisking until the mixture is smooth.

Add the broccoli, potato, and celery seed. Increase the heat to high and bring to a boil. Reduce the heat; cover and simmer, stirring occasionally, until the vegetables are tender, about 10 minutes.

Stir in the milk. When the soup is warm, add the cheese, stirring gently (taking care not to break the broccoli florets) until melted. Stir in the mustard and season to taste.

Sprinkle each serving with pepper and bread crumbs.

bread crumbs

1	tablespoon unsalted butter
1/2	cup dried caraway rye bread crumbs (see Tips)
2	tablespoons minced fresh flat-leaf parsley

soup

3	tablespoons unsalted butter
1	carrot, finely chopped
1/2	cup finely chopped onion
1/2	red bell pepper, seeded, deribbed, and finely chopped
2	cloves garlic, minced
2	tablespoons all-purpose flour
2	cups vegetable stock
1 1/2	cups small broccoli florets
1	small russet potato (about 6 ounces), peeled and cut into 1/2-inch cubes (about 1 cup)
1/4	teaspoon celery seed
2	cups milk
2	cups (8 ounces) coarsely shredded sharp Cheddar cheese (see Tips)
1/4	teaspoon dry mustard
~	salt and freshly ground pepper to taste

Refrigerate this soup and the bread crumbs in separate covered containers for up to 3 days.

TIPS

To make bread crumbs, use dry bread. Tear it into small pieces and grind it into crumbs in a food processor or blender (or put the bread in a plastic bag and crush with a rolling pin). If the bread is too moist, slice it thin and dry it in a 250° F oven, then grind into crumbs.

To store cheese, remove it from the packaging and wrap it tightly in plastic wrap or a plastic bag. Store in the refrigerator cheese compartment or another not-too-cold spot in the refrigerator for up to 2 weeks. If mold appears on firm cheese (such as Parmesan), semifirm cheese (such as Cheddar), or semisoft cheese (such as Gouda or Monterey Jack), simply cut it away. Mold on fresh or soft-ripened cheese (such as Brie or fresh white goat cheese) signals that the cheese should be thrown away.

Age is not important unless you are a cheese.
—Helen Hayes, in the play *New Woman*

asian noodle soup with spinach and corn

Vegan recipe if butter is omitted

This quick-to-prepare soup is at its best when fresh corn is available, but frozen will also do well. Offer togarashi powder (see Tips) or red pepper flakes at the table so guests may adjust the heat to taste.

Combine the vegetable stock, soy sauce, and pepper in a Dutch oven. Cover and bring to a boil over high heat.

Add the noodles, spinach, corn, and green onions. When the soup returns to a boil, cover and cook, keeping the liquid at a boil, until the noodles are tender and the spinach is wilted, about 3 minutes. As the noodles cook, stir occasionally with a fork to separate. Taste and adjust the seasoning.

To serve, use tongs to divide the noodles, spinach, and corn among the bowls, then ladle in the stock. Top each steaming bowl of soup with 1 teaspoon butter and the red pepper flakes.

advance preparation

This soup is best when prepared just before serving.

TIPS

Togarashi is a small, hot Japanese chili, available dried and ground and sold in most Asian markets. Ichimi togarashi contains only chilies. Nanomi togarashi contains the chili powder plus additional ingredients, such as sesame seeds, seaweed, and orange peel. Either can be used in recipes calling for togarashi.

Dried Chinese wheat-flour noodles are available in Asian markets and in most supermarkets. They are usually curly and tightly packed into a block; those made with eggs are yellow. Chinese noodles taste best when tender but not overcooked; they are very thin and cook quickly, so watch closely.

8	cups vegetable stock
1/4	cup soy sauce, or to taste
~	dash of ground white pepper, or to taste
4	ounces dried thin Chinese wheat-flour noodles *(see Tips)*
8	cups (about 8 ounces) stemmed and coarsely shredded fresh spinach
2	cups fresh or frozen corn kernels
2	green onions, including green parts, finely chopped
2	tablespoons salted butter
~	dash of red pepper flakes or togarashi powder, or to taste

Makes 8 cups (6 to 8 servings)

vegetarian matzo ball soup

I have fond childhood memories of matzo balls made by my favorite Jewish aunt. Matzo balls can be firm and chewy or light and fluffy, but hers, somewhere in between, were always just perfect. Of course, Aunt Ceil's traditional soup had a chicken base, which took hours to prepare. This faster vegetarian version tastes nearly as good.

to make the matzo balls

Stir together the eggs, butter, and vegetable stock in a small bowl. Add the matzo meal, parsley, dill, and 1/2 teaspoon salt; stir until evenly combined. Cover and refrigerate for at least 15 minutes or for up to 8 hours.

Bring a large pot of water to a boil over high heat; add a dash of salt. Using wet hands or a small ice-cream scoop, form the dough into 12 balls about 1 inch in diameter. Drop the balls, one at a time, into the boiling water. Reduce the heat, cover, and simmer for about 30 minutes, or until the matzo balls are plump, tender, and cooked through. (Check the stove temperature occasionally; a hard boil will break the balls apart.)

to make the soup

Combine the vegetable stock, cabbage, parsnip, bell pepper, celery and leaves, carrot, and bay leaf in a Dutch oven. Bring to a boil over high heat. Reduce the heat; cover and simmer until the vegetables are nearly tender, about 20 minutes. Stir in the remaining ingredients and cook until the vegetables are tender, about 10 minutes. Remove the bay leaf. Taste and adjust the seasoning.

When the matzo balls are done, use a slotted spoon to transfer them to a plate.

For each serving, place 2 matzo balls in a shallow soup bowl and ladle the soup over them.

matzo balls

2	eggs, lightly beaten
2	tablespoons unsalted butter, melted, or vegetable oil
2	tablespoons vegetable stock or water
1/2	cup unsalted matzo meal *(see Tips)*
1	tablespoon minced fresh flat-leaf parsley
1	tablespoon snipped fresh dill, or 1/2 teaspoon dried dill
1/2	teaspoon, plus a dash of salt

soup

6	cups vegetable stock
2	cups coarsely chopped white cabbage
1	parsnip, peeled and cut into 1/4-inch dice *(see Tips)*
1/2	red bell pepper, seeded, deribbed, and coarsely chopped
1	celery stalk with leaves, coarsely chopped
1	carrot, cut into 1/4-inch slices
1	bay leaf
1	tomato, peeled and cut into 1/2-inch dice *(see Tips, page 57)*
2	green onions, including green parts, coarsely chopped *(see Tips)*
1/4	cup coarsely chopped fresh flat-leaf parsley
~	salt and freshly ground pepper to taste

Makes 7 cups soup and 12 matzo balls
(6 servings)

advance preparation

Refrigerate this soup and the matzo balls in separate covered containers for up to 3 days. It's easiest to assemble individual servings of the soup with the matzo balls and reheat them in the microwave. Or, reheat the soup and matzo balls together in a Dutch oven for no longer than 10 minutes, taking care not to break apart the matzo balls.

TIPS

Matzo meal is made from matzo, the thin, unleavened bread traditionally eaten during Jewish Passover. Both can be found in Jewish markets as well as most supermarkets.

Parsnips are a mild, sweet-tasting white root vegetable. Look for small parsnips, up to 8 inches in length; larger roots have a stronger flavor, a fibrous texture, and a woody center. Parsnips will keep for up to 2 weeks in a plastic bag in the refrigerator; the longer they are stored, the sweeter they become. Before using, peel to remove the waxy coating.

Green onions, also called scallions, are delicate members of the onion family. Their size varies from very slender to thick; as a rule, the narrower the onion, the sweeter the flavor. The white part should be firm and unblemished; the leaves should be bright green and firm. Both parts can be used in most recipes calling for green onions. Wrap unwashed green onions in a plastic bag and store them for up to 1 week in the vegetable-crisper section of the refrigerator.

Worries go down better with soup.
—Yiddish proverb

miso soup

Vegan recipe

A culinary mainstay in Japan, miso is made with fermented soybeans mashed into a paste the consistency of peanut butter. It has a wonderful salty depth and adds texture and flavor to light, delicate vegetable soups.

Whisk together the vegetable stock and miso in a Dutch oven; add the ginger. Bring to a boil over high heat; cover and cook for about 5 minutes. Stir in the snow peas, mushrooms, carrot, green onions, and bell pepper.

Reduce the heat; cover and simmer until the vegetables are just tender, about 3 minutes. Remove the ginger and discard. Stir in the sesame oil and red pepper flakes (if using).

For each serving, ladle soup over the tofu cubes in a deep soup bowl. Garnish with the green onion curls.

advance preparation

Prepare this soup without the tofu; refrigerate in a covered container for up to 3 days. Reheat and assemble the servings with tofu.

TIPS

Miso, a Japanese condiment made from soybeans, is easily digested and highly nutritious, rich in B vitamins and protein. Look for it in Asian markets and the refrigerated section of some grocery stores, where it is sold in vacuum-sealed pouches or tubs. There are many varieties, so keep in mind that the darker the color, the stronger, saltier, and more robust the flavor will be. Store miso in the refrigerator for up to 2 years; it keeps well because of its high sodium content.

Tofu, or bean curd, is made from soybeans. The texture varies from soft to firm depending on how much water is extracted during processing. Choose extra-firm or firm tofu if you want it to hold its sliced or diced shape. Softer types are better for dips, sauces, and puddings, where a creamy consistency is desired.

6	cups vegetable stock
1/4	cup brown miso *(see Tips)*
3	1/2-inch slices fresh ginger
18	snow peas, stems and strings removed
4	large white mushrooms, thinly sliced
1	carrot, coarsely shredded
2	green onions, including green parts, finely chopped
1/4	red bell pepper, seeded, deribbed, and finely chopped
1	teaspoon Asian sesame oil *(optional)*
~	pinch of red pepper flakes, or to taste *(optional)*
6	ounces extra-firm tofu at room temperature, cut into 1/2-inch dice *(see Tips)*
~	green onion curls *(see Tips, page 101)* or sprigs of fresh cilantro for garnish

Makes 6 cups (6 servings)

greek spinach and orzo soup

Vegan recipe

Serve this light and lively lemony soup as a first course for dinner or with warm, crusty bread for lunch. Orzo is a tiny, barley-shaped pasta; riso, a similar shape, can be substituted.

Heat the oil in a Dutch oven over medium heat. Add the onion; cook, stirring occasionally, until translucent, about 5 minutes. Add the bell pepper and garlic; continue cooking, stirring occasionally, until the onion is golden and the bell pepper softens, about 5 minutes.

Add the vegetable stock and tomatoes with juice. Increase the heat to high and bring to a boil. Stir in the spinach, parsley, and orzo. Reduce the heat; cover and simmer, stirring occasionally, until the spinach is wilted and the orzo is tender, about 10 minutes. Stir in the lemon juice and season to taste.

advance preparation

Prepare this soup without adding the lemon juice. Refrigerate in a covered container for up to 5 days. When reheating, add the lemon juice and water or vegetable stock to thin as desired.

TIP

Flat-leaf, or Italian, parsley is preferable to the more common curly-leaf parsley for cooking. It has a brighter flavor and stands up to heat. Wash fresh parsley and shake off the excess moisture, then wrap the parsley in damp paper towels and store for up to 1 week in a plastic bag in the refrigerator.

2	tablespoons olive oil
1	cup coarsely chopped onion
1	red bell pepper, seeded, deribbed, and finely chopped
3	cloves garlic, minced
5	cups vegetable stock
1	15-ounce can diced tomatoes with juice
6	cups (about 6 ounces) stemmed and coarsely shredded fresh spinach
1/4	cup finely chopped fresh flat-leaf parsley *(see Tip)*
1/2	cup orzo or riso pasta
1/4	cup fresh lemon juice
~	salt and freshly ground pepper to taste

89

Makes 6 cups (4 to 6 servings)

tomato-lentil soup

Vegan recipe

I often pair this soup with crusty bread and a green salad tossed in a creamy dressing for a casual, hearty vegetarian meal. The alliance of tomatoes, lentils, and fresh herbs is very pleasing. The soup actually improves when made in advance, so that the flavors have a chance to marry.

Heat the oil in a Dutch oven over medium heat. Add the onion and garlic; cook, stirring occasionally, until the onion is translucent, about 5 minutes. Stir in the vegetable stock, lentils, carrots, celery, and bay leaf. Bring to a boil over high heat. Reduce the heat; cover and cook, stirring occasionally, until the lentils and vegetables are tender, about 1 hour.

Meanwhile, stir together the tomato paste, chopped parsley, thyme, dill, tarragon, marjoram, and pepper in a small bowl; set aside.

Remove the bay leaf from the soup. Stir in the tomatoes with juice. Add 1 cup of the soup liquid to the tomato paste mixture and stir until smooth; add to the soup and stir gently until heated through. Taste and adjust the seasoning.

Garnish each serving with a sprig of fresh herb.

90

1	tablespoon olive oil
1	cup finely chopped onion
2	cloves garlic, minced
4	cups vegetable stock
2/3	cup dried brown lentils, rinsed *(see Tip)*
2	carrots, finely chopped
2	celery stalks, finely chopped
1	bay leaf
1	6-ounce can tomato paste
1/4	cup finely chopped fresh flat-leaf parsley, plus sprigs of fresh flat-leaf parsley for garnish
1	tablespoon minced fresh thyme, or 1 teaspoon dried thyme, sprig of fresh thyme for garnish
1	tablespoon snipped fresh dill, or 1 teaspoon dried dill
1	tablespoon minced fresh tarragon, or 1 teaspoon dried tarragon
1	teaspoon minced fresh sweet marjoram, or 1/4 teaspoon dried marjoram
1/2	teaspoon freshly ground pepper, or to taste
1	28-ounce can tomatoes, coarsely chopped, with juice
~	salt to taste

This soup will keep for up to 5 days in a covered container in the refrigerator. When reheating, stir in vegetable stock or water to thin as desired.

TIP

Lentils are tiny legume seeds that were dried as soon as they ripened. All lentils have an earthy, almost nutty flavor. The most common are brown lentils, which retain their shape after cooking. Red lentils (sometimes called Egyptian lentils) are smaller and orange in their dried form. They cook quickly, fall apart, and turn bright yellow during cooking. They are found in many supermarkets and in Eastern or Indian markets.

Unlike other dried beans, lentils don't need soaking before cooking. Before using, put lentils in a colander and rinse to remove dust; also pick through them and discard any shriveled lentils or bits of gravel. You can add garlic, herbs, and spices to the lentil cooking water. Avoid adding salt and acidic ingredients, such as tomatoes, until the lentils are cooked. Adding these ingredients increases the cooking time necessary for the lentils to soften. Store lentils at room temperature in a tightly closed container, where they will keep for up to 1 year.

minestrone with white beans

Vegan recipe if cheese garnish is omitted

This is one of my favorite meals in a bowl, brimming with vegetables, pasta, and beans. Pistou, the Provençal basil-and-tomato version of pesto, transforms the humble ingredients into gastronomic gold. This minestrone is ideal as a do-ahead dinner for large groups and needs simply to be accompanied with a green salad and Sun-Dried Tomato–Goat Cheese Bruschetta (page 156) or crusty Italian bread served with Basil Pesto Butter (page 155).

Heat the oil in a Dutch oven over medium heat. Add the onion and half of the minced garlic; cook, stirring occasionally, until the onion is translucent, about 5 minutes. Add the vegetable stock, tomatoes with juice, potatoes, green beans, carrots, zucchini, and oregano. Increase the heat to high and bring to a boil. Reduce the heat; cover and simmer, stirring occasionally, until the vegetables are almost tender, about 25 minutes.

Increase the heat to high and bring to a boil. Stir in the cannellini beans and spaghetti. Reduce the heat; cover and cook until the spaghetti is tender, about 12 minutes.

Stir together the tomato paste, parsley, basil, pepper, and the remaining minced garlic; whisk into the soup. Add about $1/2$ cup of the soup liquid and stir until smooth. Gently stir this mixture into the soup. Taste and adjust the seasoning.

Ladle into large soup bowls and garnish with Parmesan.

92

3	tablespoons olive oil
1	cup finely chopped onion
4	cloves garlic, minced
5	cups vegetable stock
1	28-ounce can plum tomatoes, coarsely chopped, with juice
4	small red-skinned potatoes (about 10 ounces total), scrubbed and cut into $1/2$-inch dice (about 2 cups)
2	cups chopped green beans in 2-inch lengths (about 8 ounces)
2	carrots, cut into $1/4$-inch slices
1	zucchini, halved lengthwise and cut into $1/4$-inch slices
2	tablespoons minced fresh oregano, or 2 teaspoons dried oregano
1	15-ounce can cannellini beans, drained and rinsed *(see Tip)*
3	ounces spaghetti ($3/4$-inch bundle), broken into 2-inch pieces
1	6-ounce can tomato paste
1/4	cup finely chopped fresh flat-leaf parsley
1/4	cup finely chopped fresh basil, or 2 teaspoons dried basil
1/2	teaspoon freshly ground pepper, or to taste
~	salt to taste
~	thinly shaved Parmesan cheese for garnish

Makes 12 cups (10 to 12 servings)

advance preparation

Prepare this soup up to the step of adding the cannellini beans and spaghetti; refrigerate in a covered container for up to 3 days. Just before serving, bring the soup to a boil, add the cannellini beans and spaghetti, and complete according to the recipe. Add more vegetable stock or water to thin as desired.

variation

Substitute other beans, such as kidney beans, pinto beans, or navy beans, for the cannellini beans.

TIP

Cannellini beans are large white Italian kidney beans. In most supermarkets, they can be found either with the canned beans or with the Italian products.

At the table one never grows old.

—Italian proverb

ribollita

Vegan recipe if cheese garnish is omitted; also depending on ingredients in bread (check package label)

Ribollita, a famous Tuscan dish whose name literally means "reboiled," was originally made from leftover minestrone and day-old bread. Traditionally, the leftover soup is layered with thin slices of stale bread (or toasted bread rubbed with garlic), then simmered on the stove top or baked in the oven. This is truly comfort food, so thick you'll want to eat it with a fork, and it makes a great no-fuss family dinner on a busy night.

The Italians use salt-free Tuscan bread, which is available at some artisan bakeries. Most important is to use a bread that actually goes stale, rather than one with preservatives. Don't store the bread in plastic, where it may mold, but slice it, place it on a plate, and let it dry if necessary. Or toast it in the oven.

Recipes for ribollita vary from region to region, household to household. My friend Cynthia Myntti adapted this version from a recipe she learned while living in Siena. She recommends using more than one type of cabbage, including the traditional black cabbage, if available.

For a quicker variation of Tuscan bread soup, simply place 1 slice of stale or toasted bread in individual soup bowls and top with ladlefuls of Minestrone with White Beans (page 92).

Remove the hard stalks from the cabbage and discard. Coarsely slice the leaves; set aside.

Heat the oil in a Dutch oven over medium heat. Add the onions and minced garlic; cook, stirring occasionally, until the onions are translucent, about 5 minutes. Stir in the cabbage, tomatoes, celery, and carrots; cover and cook until the vegetables are crisp-tender, about 10 minutes. Stir in 2 cups of the stock, the tomato paste, and thyme. Increase the heat to high and bring to a boil. Reduce

1	pound savoy *(see Tip)*, black, or other cabbage, or a combination
3	tablespoons olive oil
2	onions, thinly sliced
2	cloves garlic, minced, plus 2 cloves for rubbing
3	plum tomatoes, peeled and coarsely chopped *(see Tips, page 57)*
3	celery stalks, finely chopped
3	carrots, finely chopped
6	cups vegetable stock
1	tablespoon tomato paste
1	tablespoon minced fresh thyme, or 3/4 teaspoon dried thyme
1	15-ounce can cannellini beans, drained and rinsed
~	salt and freshly ground pepper to taste
6	3/8-inch slices coarse salt-free Tuscan or other country bread (trim the crust only if it is very thick)
~	extra-virgin olive oil and freshly grated Parmesan cheese for garnish

Makes 7 cups (6 to 8 servings)

the heat; cover and simmer, stirring occasionally, for 30 minutes. Stir in the remaining 4 cups stock and the beans; cover and continue to cook for 1 hour. Season to taste.

Meanwhile, preheat the oven to 350° F. Place the bread slices on a baking sheet. Lightly toast for about 5 minutes per side, or until dry throughout. While the bread is warm, rub one side of each slice with a garlic clove.

Place the bread slices, garlic-side up, in the bottom of a large bowl. Pour the soup over the toasts; let stand until completely cool.

Before serving, return the soup and toasted bread to the Dutch oven. Bring to a boil over high heat, stirring as the bread breaks apart.

Spoon the soup into soup plates. Sprinkle each serving with pepper, drizzle with extra-virgin olive oil, and sprinkle with cheese.

advance preparation

Prepare this soup, without adding the bread, and refrigerate in a covered container for up to 3 days. When reheating, add the bread and stir until it breaks apart. Add more vegetable stock or water to thin as desired.

TIP

Savoy cabbage's crinkly, flexible green leaves grow in a loosely packed head. More tender than green cabbage and milder in flavor, its leaves are sweet, while the stems are slightly bitter. Savoy may be used interchangeably with green and red cabbage.

Food is never just something to eat.
—Margaret Visser

pumpkin stew

Vegan recipe if pumpkin is brushed with olive oil, not butter

Here's the perfect excuse to bring together a group of friends. Begin a fall day with a trip to the farmers' market, then prepare the bounty of the season and present the creation with style. Cornbread and red wine complete the fresh palette of brilliant colors and earthy flavors. If you like, garnish servings of the stew with roasted pumpkin seeds.

Heat the oil in a Dutch oven over medium heat. Add the onions and garlic; cook, stirring occasionally, until the onions are translucent, about 5 minutes. Add the tomatoes, bell pepper, potatoes, apples, and 2 cups vegetable stock. Increase the heat and bring to a boil. Reduce the heat; cover and simmer, stirring occasionally, until the vegetables are tender, about 20 minutes.

Meanwhile, preheat the oven to 325° F. Lightly oil a shallow baking pan large enough to accommodate the pumpkin. Slice off the top of the pumpkin, leaving about a 6-inch opening, and discard. Scoop out the seeds and stringy membranes, leaving the pumpkin flesh intact; brush the inside and top edge with the melted butter and sprinkle lightly with salt and pepper. Place the shell in the prepared baking pan.

Stir the stew and add the black beans, sherry, 1/2 teaspoon salt, and 1/2 teaspoon pepper. Pour the mixture into the pumpkin shell. Bake for about 1 hour and 15 minutes, or until the pumpkin flesh is fork tender. (Thicker pumpkins will take longer, up to 1 1/2 hours.)

Carefully transfer the pumpkin to a large bowl. (Take special care, because the shell may be soft in places.) If the stew has become too thick to suit you, gently stir in some hot vegetable stock.

continued . . .

2	tablespoons olive oil
1 1/2	cups coarsely chopped onions
4	cloves garlic, minced
2	large tomatoes, cut into 1/2-inch dice
1	red bell pepper, seeded, deribbed, and coarsely chopped
1	russet potato (about 10 ounces), peeled and cut into 1/2-inch dice (about 2 cups)
1	orange-fleshed sweet potato (about 12 ounces), peeled and cut into 1/2-inch dice (about 2 cups; *see Tips, page 98*)
1	cup dried apple slices
2	cups vegetable stock, plus more as needed
1	sugar (pie) pumpkin (8 to 10 pounds; *see Tips, page 98*)
2	tablespoons unsalted butter, melted
~	salt for sprinkling, plus 1/2 teaspoon
~	freshly ground pepper for sprinkling, plus 1/2 teaspoon
1	15-ounce can black beans, drained and rinsed
1/4	cup dry sherry (*see Tip, page 36*)

Makes 8 cups and pumpkin
(6 to 8 servings)

96

For each serving, use a large spoon to scoop out a wedge of cooked pumpkin; place in the bottom of a soup bowl. Top with the stew.

advance preparation

Cook this stew on the stove early the day it is to be served; refrigerate in a covered container. Bake it in the pumpkin just before serving. Refrigerate the leftover soup and baked pumpkin flesh scooped from the shell in separate covered containers for up to 5 days; discard the pumpkin shell.

variations

~ To shorten baking time, clean and season the pumpkin; bake it for 30 minutes while making the stew. Bake for 45 to 60 minutes after filling with the stew.

~ Rather than baking the stew in one large pumpkin, bake about $1^{1}/_{3}$ cups of the stew in each of 6 single-serving sugar pumpkins, each weighing about 2 pounds and measuring 6 inches in diameter. Reduce the baking time to about 1 hour, or until the pumpkin flesh is fork tender.

~ Serve the stew in Roasted Acorn Squash Soup Bowls (page 152) rather than in the pumpkin.

~ For a simpler presentation, cook the stew on the stove top, simmering it uncovered until the desired consistency. Serve in soup bowls.

TIPS

What is labeled a "yam" at the supermarket most likely is an orange sweet potato. These have a dark, uniformly colored brown skin, a shape that tapers on both ends, a bright orange flesh, and a sweet flavor when cooked. White sweet potatoes have a lighter, thinner skin, pale yellow flesh, and a less-sweet flavor. Store sweet potatoes in a cool, dry, dark, and well-ventilated place for up to 2 weeks; do not refrigerate.

The best cooking pumpkins are sugar, or pie, pumpkins, which were developed for pie making. Avoid field, or jack-o'-lantern, pumpkins for cooking; they are usually fibrous and flavorless. Fresh pumpkins are available in the fall and early winter; they will keep at room temperature for up to 1 month or in the refrigerator for up to 3 months.

indian cumin-scented coconut milk stew with basmati rice

Vegan recipe

From the coastal areas of southern India, this aromatic and comforting stew is a family favorite of my friend and fellow cookbook author Raghavan Iyer. The dish represents the distinctive flavors of his homeland with plenty of coriander, cumin, and hot chilies.

to cook the rice

    Combine all the ingredients in a saucepan with a tight-fitting lid. Bring to a boil over high heat; stir once. Reduce the heat; cover and simmer until the liquid is absorbed, about 15 minutes, or according to package instructions. Remove from the heat and let stand, covered, for about 10 minutes.

to make the stew

    Heat the oil in a Dutch oven over medium heat. Add the onion and garlic; cook, stirring occasionally, until the onion is translucent, about 5 minutes.

    Add the coriander and cumin; stir for about 30 seconds. Add the potato and bell pepper; continue cooking, stirring occasionally, until the vegetables are crisp-tender, about 3 minutes.

    Stir in the coconut milk, water, chickpeas, and spinach. Increase the heat to high and bring to a boil. Reduce the heat; cover and simmer until the potato is tender, about 5 minutes.

    Stir in all the cilantro and chilies; cover and continue to simmer for 5 to 7 minutes to blend flavors. Season to taste.

    To serve, fluff the rice with a fork. Spread a layer of rice in the bottom of shallow soup plates and top with the stew. Garnish with green onion curls.

continued . . .

rice

1   cup basmati rice
(see Tips, page 101)

1¹⁄₂   cups water

~   salt to taste

stew

1   tablespoon canola oil

1   cup finely chopped onion

4   cloves garlic, minced

1   tablespoon ground coriander

1   teaspoon ground cumin

1   russet potato (about 10 ounces), peeled and cut into ¹⁄₂-inch dice (about 2 cups)

¹⁄₂   red bell pepper, seeded, deribbed, and coarsely chopped

1   14-ounce can "lite" coconut milk *(see Tips, page 101)*

1   cup water

1   15-ounce can chickpeas (garbanzo beans), drained and rinsed

10   cups (about 10 ounces) stemmed and coarsely chopped fresh spinach

2   tablespoons minced fresh cilantro

2   fresh serrano chilies, minced (about 4 teaspoons), or to taste

¹⁄₂   teaspoon salt, or to taste

~   green onion curls *(see Tips, page 101)* for garnish

Makes 6 cups (4 to 6 servings)

advance preparation

Refrigerate this stew and the rice in separate covered containers for up to 3 days.

TIPS

True basmati rice, the famous aged aromatic rice, is grown in the foothills of the Himalayan Mountains; less aromatic varieties are grown in the United States, primarily in the Southwest and California. In both brown and white forms, it has a nutlike fragrance and a delicate, almost-buttery flavor. Lower in starch than other long-grain rices, basmati rice grains cook up fluffy and separate. Store basmati rice in an airtight container in a cool, dry place for up to 1 year.

Do not confuse canned unsweetened coconut milk with "cream of coconut," used mainly for desserts and mixed drinks. Low-fat, or "lite," coconut milk, available in Asian markets and some supermarkets, contains about half the calories and fat of regular coconut milk. To reduce the fat when using regular coconut milk, combine it with an equal amount of water. In both low-fat and regular products, the coconut fat naturally separates from the coconut milk; shake well before using.

To make green onion curls, slice the green parts of green onions very thinly lengthwise. Drop into a bowl of ice water; curls will form in 10 to 15 minutes.

No treasure is equal to rice.

—Indian proverb

moroccan red lentil–bean stew

Vegan recipe

In Morocco, a well-loved stew called *harira* breaks religious fasts. Each household has its own version. This recipe, a creation of my friend and chef extraordinaire Nathan Fong, replaces the traditional lamb or beef with plenty of white beans. It's a satisfying, hearty meal.

Heat the oil in a Dutch oven over medium heat. Add the onion; cook, stirring occasionally, until translucent, about 5 minutes.

Meanwhile, mix the saffron with the hot water; set aside.

Add the curry powder, cumin, rosemary, and fennel seeds to the Dutch oven; stir for about 30 seconds. Stir in the saffron mixture and the vegetable stock, beans, lentils, and rice. Increase the heat to high and bring to a boil. Reduce the heat; cover and simmer, stirring occasionally, until the lentils and rice are tender, about 30 minutes. Stir in the tomato, chopped cilantro, and tomato paste. Season to taste.

Garnish servings with sprigs of cilantro.

advance preparation

This stew will keep for up to 5 days in a covered container in the refrigerator. When reheating, stir in vegetable stock or water to thin as desired.

variation

Substitute brown lentils for the red lentils; increase the cooking time to about 35 minutes, or until the lentils are tender.

TIP

Fennel seeds, which add a mild licorice flavor to both sweet and savory foods, are available whole or ground. Like other seeds, they should be stored in a cool, dark place for up to 6 months.

1	tablespoon olive oil
1	cup finely chopped onion
1	teaspoon saffron threads, crushed (*see Tip, page 106*)
1	tablespoon hot water
2	teaspoons curry powder
1	teaspoon ground cumin
2	teaspoons minced fresh rosemary, or 1 teaspoon dried rosemary, crushed (*see Tips, page 115*)
1	teaspoon fennel seeds (*see Tip*)
6	cups vegetable stock, heated
1	15-ounce can white beans, drained and rinsed
1/2	cup dried red lentils
1/2	cup basmati rice
1	tomato, cut into 1/2-inch dice
1/3	cup coarsely chopped fresh cilantro, plus sprigs of fresh cilantro for garnish
1	tablespoon tomato paste
~	few drops of Tabasco sauce, or to taste
~	salt and freshly ground pepper to taste

Makes 5 cups (4 to 6 servings)

mediterranean saffron stew with rouille

Vegan recipe

This is a vegetarian version of the seafood soups that are classics of Mediterranean cuisine. Three different kinds of potatoes lend their unique earthy flavors to the soup. Top the servings with rouille, the traditional rust-colored, peppery Provençal sauce.

to make the rouille

Put the bread crumbs in a bowl and sprinkle with the water; squeeze until crumbly and dry. Blend the crumbs with all the remaining ingredients in a small food processor or blender, pushing down the sides occasionally, until smooth. Transfer to a covered container and set aside at room temperature to allow the flavors to blend.

to make the soup

Mix the saffron with the hot water; set aside.

Heat the oil in a Dutch oven or large pot over medium heat. Add the onion and garlic; cook, stirring occasionally, until the onion is translucent, about 5 minutes. Stir in the saffron mixture and all the remaining ingredients, except the parsley and salt. Increase the heat to high and bring to a boil. Reduce the heat; cover and simmer, stirring occasionally, until the vegetables are tender, about 10 minutes. Stir in the parsley and salt; taste and adjust the seasoning.

Top each serving with a dollop of rouille.

continued . . .

rouille

1/4 cup dried bread crumbs (see Tip, page 83)

1 tablespoon water

1/4 cup coarsely chopped jarred roasted red bell pepper

3 tablespoons extra-virgin olive oil

2 teaspoons minced fresh red chili, or to taste

2 teaspoons fresh lemon juice

1 teaspoon capers, drained and rinsed

2 cloves garlic, minced

1/8 teaspoon salt

soup

1/4 teaspoon saffron threads, crushed (see Tip, page 106)

1 tablespoon hot water

2 tablespoons olive oil

1 cup finely chopped onion

4 cloves garlic, minced

6 cups vegetable stock

3 small red-skinned potatoes (about 6 ounces total), scrubbed and cut into 1/2-inch dice

1 Yukon Gold potato (about 8 ounces), scrubbed and cut into 1/2-inch dice (about 1 1/2 cups)

1 small orange-fleshed sweet potato (about 8 ounces), peeled and cut into 1/2-inch dice (about 1 1/2 cups)

Makes 10 cups (8 servings)

advance preparation

Refrigerate this soup and the rouille in separate covered containers for up to 5 days. Before serving, bring the rouille to room temperature.

variation

Substitute Roasted Red Pepper Coulis (page 64) for the rouille.

TIP

Saffron, the yellow-orange stigmas of a small purple crocus, is the world's most expensive spice. Each flower provides only three stigmas, which must be handpicked, and it takes fourteen thousand of these to equal 1 ounce of saffron. There is no substitute for its exquisite flavor and earthy aroma. Powdered saffron loses its flavor more readily and can easily be adulterated with less expensive powders like turmeric, so purchase whole saffron threads. Heat releases the flavor, so soak the threads in hot water (or milk, depending on the recipe) before using. Store saffron in an airtight container in a cool, dark place for up to 6 months.

Salt is born of the purest of parents:
the sun and the sea.

—Pythegoras

2	large tomatoes, peeled and coarsely chopped *(see Tips, page 57)*
1	carrot, finely chopped
1	celery stalk, finely chopped
1	teaspoon minced fresh red chili, or $1/8$ teaspoon red pepper flakes, or to taste
1/2	teaspoon freshly ground pepper, or to taste
1/4	cup finely chopped fresh flat-leaf parsley
1/2	teaspoon salt, or to taste

cashew-carrot stew

Vegan recipe

A family favorite for years, this is fun to serve friends, who are always surprised to find raisins and cashews in their stew. For their visual appeal and texture, use whole cashews, rather than the less expensive halved or broken ones.

Heat the oil in a Dutch oven over medium heat. Add the cabbage, carrots, and onion; cook, stirring occasionally, until the carrots are tender, about 10 minutes.

Meanwhile, whisk together the vegetable stock and tomato paste in a measuring cup; add to the soup pot. Increase the heat to high and bring to a boil. Stir in the apple and rice. Reduce the heat; cover and simmer until the rice is tender but firm, about 35 minutes.

Stir in the raisins and cashews. Cover and cook, stirring occasionally, until the rice is tender and the raisins are plumped, about 10 minutes. Season to taste.

advance preparation

This stew will keep for up to 5 days in a covered container in the refrigerator. When reheating, stir in vegetable stock or water to thin as desired.

TIP

Choose a heavy head of cabbage with fresh, bright, firm leaves. Tightly wrapped in plastic and refrigerated, it will keep for up to 1 week.

To shred cabbage, remove the outer leaves and the core. Cut the head into 4 to 8 pieces through the stem end. Place a wedge, flat-side down, on a cutting board. Hold the cabbage by its stem end and slice it in straight 1/8-inch slices. As the slices fall, they will break into thin shreds. To shred in a food processor, run the wedges through the feed tube, shredding with the slicing disk.

2	tablespoons olive oil
2	cups finely shredded white cabbage *(see Tip)*
2	cups finely chopped carrots
1	cup finely chopped onion
6	cups vegetable stock
1/4	cup tomato paste
1	apple, cored, peeled, and cut into 1/2-inch chunks
1/3	cup long-grain brown rice
1/2	cup dark raisins
1/2	cup whole raw cashews
~	salt and freshly ground pepper to taste

acorn squash and fava bean stew with bulgur wheat

Vegan recipe if cheese garnish is omitted

Vegetarian comfort food at its best, this stew is chunky and aromatic. For a hearty dinner in a bowl, serve it over bulgur wheat, a nutritional whole-grain powerhouse.

to cook the bulgur wheat

Bring the water to a boil in a medium saucepan over high heat. Stir in the bulgur and salt. Reduce the heat; cover and simmer for 10 minutes. Remove from the heat and let stand for 15 minutes. Or, prepare according to package instructions. Drain if necessary.

to make the soup

Heat the oil in a Dutch oven over medium heat. Add the onion and garlic; cook, stirring occasionally, until the onion is translucent, about 8 minutes. Add the cumin; stir for about 30 seconds. Stir in the vegetable stock, tomatoes and juice, squash, beans, and red pepper flakes. Bring to a boil over high heat. Reduce the heat; cover and simmer, stirring occasionally, until the squash is almost tender, about 8 minutes.

Stir in the chard; cover and cook until it is wilted and the squash is tender, about 5 minutes. Season to taste.

To serve, fluff the bulgur with a fork and spoon into the bottom of serving bowls. Top with the stew and garnish with cheese.

108

bulgur wheat

3	cups water
1	cup bulgur wheat
1/2	teaspoon salt

soup

1	tablespoon olive oil
1	large yellow onion, cut into 1/4-inch wedges
4	cloves garlic, minced
1	teaspoon ground cumin
2	cups vegetable stock
1	15-ounce can diced tomatoes with juice
1	2-pound acorn squash, peeled, seeded, and cut into 1-inch chunks (about 5 cups)
1	19-ounce can fava beans, drained and rinsed *(see Tips)*
1/4	teaspoon red pepper flakes
4	cups coarsely shredded Swiss chard leaves *(see Tips)*
~	salt and freshly ground pepper to taste
~	thin slivers of Parmesan cheese for garnish

advance preparation

Refrigerate this stew and the bulgur wheat in separate containers for up to 5 days.

variation

Substitute couscous for the bulgur wheat: Combine 1 1/2 cups vegetable stock and 1 1/2 cups couscous according to the instructions on page 110.

TIPS

Fava beans are shaped like very large lima beans. They can be purchased dried in some natural-foods stores or canned in many supermarkets. Fava beans are popular in Mediterranean and Middle Eastern dishes.

Swiss chard is grown for its crinkly green leaves and silvery, celerylike stalks. The greens are prepared like spinach, the stalks like asparagus. The variety with dark green leaves and reddish stalks has a stronger flavor. Store unwashed chard, wrapped in a plastic bag, in the refrigerator for up to 3 days.

summer stew with couscous

Vegan recipe if cheese garnish is omitted

An uncomplicated recipe for prolific gardeners, or their friends who have been awarded their summer bounty. Feel free to add or substitute other vegetables, such as green beans, corn, peas, or whatever is in overflowing supply. And so the tender vegetables won't be overcooked, it's best to make this just before serving.

to prepare the couscous

Pour the vegetable stock into a medium saucepan; bring to a boil over high heat. Stir in the couscous; cover the pan and remove it from the heat. Let stand for about 5 minutes or until the liquid is completely absorbed.

to make the stew

Heat the oil in a large sauté pan over medium heat. Add the onion; cook, stirring occasionally, until translucent, about 5 minutes. Stir in the vegetable stock; bring to a boil over medium–high heat. Reduce the heat to medium; stir in the zucchini, yellow squash, tomatoes, garlic, and oregano. Cover and simmer, stirring occasionally, until the vegetables are tender but not mushy, about 5 minutes. Stir in the basil and season to taste.

Fluff the couscous with a fork. Stir in the parsley and olive oil; season to taste.

To serve, spread couscous in the bottom of shallow soup plates, top with the stew, and sprinkle with cheese.

continued . . .

continued . . .

couscous

1½ cups vegetable stock

1½ cups couscous *(see Tip, page 112)*

stew

1 tablespoon olive oil

1 Vidalia or other sweet onion, coarsely chopped (about 2 cups)

2 cups vegetable stock

2 zucchini, halved lengthwise and cut into ¼-inch slices

2 yellow squash, halved lengthwise and cut into ¼-inch slices

2 large tomatoes, cut into 1-inch cubes

6 cloves garlic, minced

2 teaspoons minced fresh oregano

½ cup coarsely chopped fresh basil

to complete the recipe

¼ cup finely chopped fresh flat-leaf parsley

1 tablespoon extra-virgin olive oil

~ salt and freshly ground pepper to taste

~ freshly grated pecorino Romano cheese for garnish

Makes 6 cups (6 servings)

advance preparation

This stew and the couscous are best when prepared just before serving.

variation

When substituting vegetables, keep in mind that firmer vegetables will take longer to cook, so be sure to add them first.

TIP

Couscous, sometimes called Moroccan pasta, is a tiny, beadlike pasta made from semolina flour. It is available both in white and whole-wheat varieties in most supermarkets. It keeps almost indefinitely in a tightly closed container in a dark, dry place.

roasted vegetable stew

Vegan recipe if cheese garnish is omitted

Roasting intensifies the flavors of vegetables and brings out their natural sweetness in this simple stew flavored with robust herbs (see Tips, page 115). I like to serve it in pasta bowls. Spoon the stew over wide egg noodles, or substitute mashed potatoes.

Preheat the oven to 425° F. Stir together the oil, garlic, oregano, rosemary, thyme, 1/4 teaspoon pepper, and 1/4 teaspoon salt in a large bowl. Add the vegetables and toss until coated. Transfer the vegetables to a roasting pan. Bake, uncovered, turning the vegetables occasionally, for about 30 minutes, or until tender.

Bring a medium pot of water to a boil over high heat.

When the vegetables are done, transfer the roasting pan to the stove top. Stir in the vegetable stock, tomato paste, and tomatoes. Cover and cook over medium heat for about 15 minutes. Season to taste.

When the water comes to a boil, add salt, then the noodles. Reduce the heat; cook for about 5 to 7 minutes, or according to package instructions, until noodles are firm but cooked through. Drain well.

To serve, spread noodles in the bottom of pasta bowls. Top with the stew; garnish with pepper and feta cheese.

continued . . .

3	tablespoons olive oil
4	cloves garlic, minced
1	teaspoon minced fresh oregano *(see Tips, page 115)*
1	teaspoon minced fresh rosemary *(see Tips, page 115)*
1	teaspoon minced fresh thyme *(see Tips, page 115)*
1/4	teaspoon freshly ground pepper, or to taste
1/4	teaspoon salt, or to taste
8	ounces asparagus spears, trimmed and cut into 1-inch lengths (about 2 cups)
1	cup baby carrots, halved horizontally
1	red bell pepper, seeded, deribbed, and cut into 1½-by-½-inch strips
1	small zucchini, halved lengthwise and cut into ½-inch slices
1/2	red onion, cut into ½-inch wedges
1¼	cups vegetable stock
2	tablespoons tomato paste *(see Tips, page 115)*
2	tomatoes, each cut into 8 wedges
2	cups (about 4 ounces) wide egg noodles
~	crumbled feta cheese for garnish

113

Makes 4 cups (4 servings)

advance preparation

This stew will keep for up to 5 days in a covered container in the refrigerator. When reheating, thin with water as desired. Prepare the noodles or mashed potatoes just before serving.

variation

If you don't have a roasting pan, roast the vegetables on a jelly-roll pan lined with aluminum foil. Transfer the vegetables to a Dutch oven to finish cooking the stew on the stove top.

TIPS

Thyme, savory, bay leaf, rosemary, sage, oregano, and marjoram are considered to be the "robust herbs," with tough leaves that are resistant to cold weather and to heat—of the sun and of cooking. They are strong in aroma and hearty in flavor, so add them early in the cooking process to give them time to mellow and blend in with the other ingredients. Add tender herbs, such as basil, cilantro, dill, and parsley, toward the end of the cooking time, or sprinkle them on top of the completed dish.

Rosemary has a bold taste, so use it sparingly. To enhance the flavor and reduce the splintery texture of dried rosemary, crush the leaves between your fingers just before adding to a dish. When mincing fresh herbs with twiglike stems, such as rosemary and thyme, use only the leaves and tender tips.

Concentrated tomato paste is available in tubes, ideal for recipes calling for less than a 6-ounce can. Refrigerate the tube after opening.

spicy green bean and potato stew

Vegan recipe if cheese garnish is omitted

This spicy Greek vegetable dish is traditionally served at room temperature with thick slices of crusty bread. I think it's even better warm, garnished generously with feta cheese.

Heat the oil in a large sauté pan over medium heat. Add the onion; cook, stirring occasionally, until translucent, about 5 minutes. Add the green beans; continue to cook, stirring constantly, until the onion is tender, about 5 minutes.

Stir in the tomatoes and juice, zucchini, potato, water, pepper, and cayenne pepper. Increase the heat to high and bring to a boil. Reduce the heat; cover and simmer, stirring occasionally, until the green beans and potatoes are tender, about 40 minutes.

Stir in the parsley and salt, keeping in mind that the feta cheese garnish is salty in flavor. Taste and adjust the seasoning.

Top each serving with a generous amount of feta cheese.

advance preparation

If possible, prepare this stew 1 day in advance to allow the flavors to blend; cover and refrigerate for up to 5 days. Bring to room temperature or heat, stirring gently and taking care not to break the potatoes, before serving.

TIP

Feta cheese is a white Greek cheese with a rich, tangy flavor. Traditionally, it is made with goat's milk, sheep's milk, or a combination; today it is also often made with cow's milk. In some markets, you will find varieties flavored with peppercorns or herbs. Feta is crumbly when fresh, drier and saltier when mature.

2	tablespoons olive oil
1	cup coarsely chopped onion
4	cups chopped green beans in 2-inch lengths (about 1 pound)
1	28-ounce can plum (Italian) tomatoes, with juice
2	zucchini, halved lengthwise and cut into 1/2-inch slices
1	large russet potato (about 12 ounces), peeled and cut into 1-inch cubes (about 2 cups)
1/4	cup water
1/2	teaspoon freshly ground pepper, or to taste
1/4	teaspoon cayenne pepper, or to taste
1/2	cup finely chopped fresh flat-leaf parsley
~	salt to taste
~	crumbled plain feta or peppercorn feta cheese *(see Tip)* for garnish

Makes 8 cups (6 to 8 servings)

egyptian split-pea stew

Vegan recipe if yogurt garnish is omitted

This hearty but simple stew, spiked with red pepper and lively with cilantro and dill, makes an easy supper. My well-traveled friend Cynthia Myntti, who introduced this recipe to me, recommends serving it over fragrant basmati rice and topping the dish with thickened yogurt.

to make the stew

Heat the oil in a Dutch oven over medium heat. Add the onion and garlic; cook, stirring occasionally, until the onion is translucent, about 5 minutes.

Add 3 cups of the vegetable stock. Increase the heat to high and bring to a boil. Stir in the split peas. Reduce the heat; cover and simmer until the split peas are tender but not mushy, about 50 minutes. During the last 15 minutes, stir in the remaining 1 cup vegetable stock, the tomatoes, spinach, cilantro, parsley, dill, red pepper flakes, salt, and pepper. Taste and adjust the seasoning.

to cook the rice

During the last 30 minutes, put all the ingredients in a saucepan with a tight-fitting lid. Bring to a boil over high heat; stir once. Reduce the heat; cover and simmer until the liquid is absorbed, about 15 minutes, or according to the package instructions. Remove from the heat and let stand, covered, for about 10 minutes.

To serve, fluff the rice with a fork. Spread a layer of rice in the bottom of shallow soup plates; top with the stew and garnish with yogurt.

continued . . .

stew

2	tablespoons olive oil
1	cup coarsely chopped onion
8	cloves garlic, minced
4	cups vegetable stock
1½	cups split peas *(see Tips, page 119)*
4	large ripe tomatoes, peeled and coarsely chopped *(see Tips, page 57)*
8	cups (about 8 ounces) stemmed and coarsely chopped fresh spinach
½	cup finely chopped fresh cilantro
½	cup finely chopped fresh flat-leaf parsley
2	tablespoons snipped fresh dill, or 1 teaspoon dried dill
¼	teaspoon red pepper flakes, or to taste
~	salt and freshly ground pepper to taste

rice

2	cups basmati rice
3	cups water
~	salt to taste
~	plain yogurt or thickened plain yogurt *(see Tips, page 119)* for garnish

117

Makes 8 cups (6 to 8 servings)

Refrigerate this stew and the rice in separate covered containers for up to 5 days. When reheating, add vegetable stock or water to thin as desired.

TIPS

Split peas, or field peas, are a variety of peas grown specifically for drying. When dried, they split along a natural seam, which gives them their name. You'll find them in most supermarkets. Store split peas in a sealed container in a cool, dry place for up to 1 year. Pick through them before using to discard any discolored or shriveled peas or small pebbles. There is no need to presoak split peas before cooking.

To thicken yogurt, set a sieve over a deep bowl, making certain the sieve does not touch the bottom of the bowl. Line the sieve with 4 layers of cheesecloth, allowing about 4 inches to extend over the sides of the sieve. Spoon the yogurt into the sieve. Gather the ends of the cheesecloth and fold them over the yogurt. Cover the sieve with plastic wrap to prevent the surface from drying out. Refrigerate for at least 8 hours or overnight. Transfer the thickened yogurt to a covered container; discard the cheesecloth and liquid. Refrigerate the thickened yogurt in a covered container for up to 1 week.

chilled soups

In summer heat, when food must be fast, light, and cooling, soups are perfect. Make them ahead in the morning, then refrigerate all day to let the flavors develop.

These soups can be served as tasty first courses, as side dishes to accompany soups or salads, or as a light main course accompanied with bread. Lettuce Soup with Radish Salsa (page 127) makes a surprising addition to a summer brunch.

Remember that some cooked foods lessen in flavor as they chill, and herbs and spices will blend with the other ingredients and become subtler after a day in the refrigerator. So be sure to taste a spoonful and adjust the seasoning just before serving.

There is little fat in most chilled soups, and many are uncooked. This means that the ingredients must be garden fresh, so use only the best. Serve most of these soups within a day, or two at the most, for top-notch flavor.

As a special touch, present cool creations in chilled bowls. To be fancy, place the soup bowls inside larger bowls filled with crushed ice.

Steep thyself in a bowl of summertime.
—William Shakespeare

carrot vichyssoise with sweet balsamic swirls

Chef Louis Diat at the Ritz-Carlton Hotel in New York created classic vichys-soise in the 1920s. Here, carrots add color, and swirls of balsamic reduction garnish the rich, velvety soup for a stunning presentation. Reducing balsamic with dark molasses gives it the thick, syrupy sweet richness of pricey imported aged balsamics.

to make the soup

Combine the vegetable stock, potato, carrots, and leek in a Dutch oven. Bring to a boil over high heat. Reduce the heat; cover and simmer until the vegetables are very tender, about 25 minutes.

In 2 batches, purée the soup in a blender until smooth. Transfer to a bowl and stir in the half-and-half. Season generously to taste.

Refrigerate in a covered container until chilled, at least 4 hours, before serving.

to prepare the balsamic reduction

Combine the vinegar and molasses in a small saucepan. Bring to a simmer over medium heat; cook, stirring occasionally, until the amount is reduced by about half and the mixture is a maple-syrup consistency, about 8 minutes. Transfer to a bowl. Cover and refrigerate; the mixture will continue to thicken as it cools.

Drizzle each cup of soup with a swirl of the balsamic reduction.

continued . . .

soup

3 cups vegetable stock

1 large russet potato (about 12 ounces), peeled and diced (about 2¼ cups)

1¼ cups thinly sliced carrots

1 leek (white part only), halved lengthwise, rinsed, and thinly sliced

1 cup half-and-half

~ salt and ground white pepper to taste

balsamic reduction

½ cup balsamic vinegar *(see Tip, page 124)*

1 tablespoon dark molasses

Makes 4 cups (4 to 6 servings)

122

Refrigerate this soup and the balsamic reduction in separate covered containers for up to 3 days. Before serving, stir in half-and-half, vegetable stock, or water to thin the soup as desired. If necessary, add water to thin the balsamic reduction.

TIP

Balsamic vinegar, the Italian *aceto balsamico,* is wine vinegar made by boiling the juice of white Trebbiano grapes in copper pots until it caramelizes. The vinegar is then aged for up to one hundred years in barrels made from various woods (oak, chestnut, mulberry, and juniper), each adding a hint of its woody flavor and color. The result is a vinegar with a heavy, mellow, almost-sweet flavor, and a dark color. Store balsamic vinegar in a cool, dark place for up to 6 months after opening.

Some commercial balsamic vinegars are made from red wine vinegar that has been fortified with concentrated grape juice and caramelized sugar. They can be used in recipes but lack the flavor complexity of true *aceto balsamico tradizionale*.

Carrots in a dream prophesy an unexpected legacy or money windfall.
—*The Dreamer's Dictionary*

roasted red beet and carrot borscht

To allow time for the flavors to blend, this brilliantly colored soup should be made a day before serving. I like to serve it chilled, but it's also delicious warm.

Preheat the oven to 350° F.

Wrap 3 of the beets tightly in separate squares of aluminum foil. Place them on a baking sheet and roast until tender when pierced with a knife, about 1 hour.

Meanwhile, cut the remaining 3 beets into 1-inch pieces. (It's not necessary to peel them first.)

Heat the oil in a Dutch oven over medium heat; add the just-cut beets, the cabbage, carrot, leeks, and garlic; cook until the vegetables are partially tender, about 5 minutes. Add the vegetable stock, peppercorns, cloves, and bay leaf. Increase the heat to high and bring to a boil. Reduce the heat; cover and simmer, stirring occasionally, for 1 hour.

When the roasted beets are done, remove them from the oven and let cool. Rub off the skins under cool running water. Cut the beets into 1/2-inch dice.

Drain the beet liquid through a fine-meshed sieve over a medium bowl; discard the solids. Whisk in the 3/4 cup sour cream. Stir in the brown sugar, vinegar, and the diced roasted beets. Season to taste.

Refrigerate in a covered container until chilled, at least 4 hours, before serving.

Garnish each serving with a sprinkling of pepper and a swirl of sour cream topped with dill.

continued . . .

6	red beets, scrubbed, greens trimmed to 1 inch *(see Tip)*
1	tablespoon canola oil
2	cups coarsely shredded white cabbage *(see Tip, page 107)*
1	cup coarsely shredded carrot
2	leeks (white parts only), halved lengthwise, rinsed, and cut into 1/4-inch slices
2	cloves garlic, minced
5	cups vegetable stock
1	tablespoon whole black peppercorns
2	whole cloves
1	bay leaf
3/4	cup sour cream, plus more for garnish
1	tablespoon packed light brown sugar
1	tablespoon sherry vinegar
~	salt to taste
~	freshly ground pepper and snipped fresh dill for garnish

125

Makes 4 cups (4 to 6 servings)

Refrigerate this soup for up to 3 days in a covered container. Serve chilled or reheat, taking care not to let the mixture come to a boil (the sour cream may separate).

TIP

To prepare beets for cooking, trim off all but 1 inch of the greens and leave the root end intact. Scrub the beets well, but do not break the skin; then dry. To avoid staining your hands and cutting board when working with cooked beets, wear disposable plastic or latex gloves, slip off the skins under cool running water, and protect the cutting board with plastic wrap or waxed paper.

Borscht and bread make your cheeks red.

—Jewish proverb

lettuce soup with radish salsa

A lovely emerald green, this soup is as light and refreshing as a garden salad. It makes a splashy start to any summer meal, especially dressed up with its peppery salsa.

to make the soup

Purée all the soup ingredients, except the salt and pepper, in a blender until smooth. Season to taste.

Refrigerate in a covered container until chilled, at least 3 hours, before serving. Taste and adjust the seasoning.

to make the salsa

Whisk together the olive oil, vinegar, sugar, mustard, salt, and pepper in a small bowl. Stir in the radish and cucumber strips. Cover and refrigerate.

Serve the soup in shallow bowls with a mound of the salsa spooned atop each serving.

continued . . .

soup

4 cups torn butterhead lettuce leaves *(see Tips, page 129)*

2 cups (about 2 ounces) stemmed baby spinach

1 cup fresh flat-leaf parsley sprigs

1/3 cup coarsely chopped shallot *(see Tips, page 129)*

3/4 cup plain yogurt

2 tablespoons fresh lemon juice

2 cups vegetable stock

~ salt and freshly ground pepper to taste

salsa

1 tablespoon extra-virgin olive oil

1 tablespoon red wine vinegar

1/2 teaspoon sugar

1/8 teaspoon dry mustard

~ dash of salt and freshly ground pepper

1/4 cup red radish matchsticks (1-by-1/8-inch strips)

1/4 cup seeded-cucumber matchsticks (1-by-1/8-inch strips)

Makes 4 cups (4 servings)

advance preparation

Refrigerate this soup and the salsa for up to 2 days in separate covered containers.

variation

Top the servings with Herbed Garlic Croutons (page 150) rather than radish salsa.

TIPS

Butterhead, or butter, lettuces have soft, buttery-textured, sweet-flavored leaves in small, round, loosely formed heads. Boston and Bibb are two of the best-known varieties.

Shallots, a member of the onion family, are small bulbous herbs with a mild onion-garlic flavor. Dehydrated products will not do; always use fresh shallots. (If unavailable, substitute some fresh onion and garlic.) Fresh shallots will keep for up to 1 month in the bottom bin of your refrigerator; use before they become wrinkled or begin to sprout. When cooking, don't allow shallots to brown or they will taste bitter.

avocado soup with orange marmalade chutney

This blend of ingredients is an example of combining sweet, salty, acidic, and hot. The uncooked soup is delicious on its own, but with the topping it's decidedly memorable. Serve in small portions as a first course rather than as a main course.

to make the soup

Purée all the ingredients in a blender until smooth. Refrigerate in a covered container until chilled, at least 3 hours, before serving.

to make the chutney

Stir together all the ingredients in a small bowl; taste and adjust the seasoning. Cover and refrigerate.

To serve, thin the soup with more vegetable stock as desired. Taste and adjust the seasoning. Drizzle each serving with about 1 tablespoon of the chutney mixture.

soup

2	ripe avocados, peeled, pitted, and coarsely chopped *(see Tip)*
1	cup vegetable stock, or more as needed
1	cup fresh orange juice
1/2	cup plain yogurt
1/4	cup fresh cilantro leaves
1/4	cup finely chopped red onion
1	tablespoon thin strips orange zest *(see Tips)*
1	tablespoon minced fresh ginger
2	cloves garlic, minced
~	pinch of red pepper flakes, or to taste
~	salt and freshly ground pepper to taste

chutney

3	tablespoons orange marmalade
2	teaspoons red wine vinegar
1	tablespoon minced red onion
1	clove garlic, minced
1/8	teaspoon red pepper flakes, or to taste
1/8	teaspoon salt, or to taste

Makes 4 cups (4 to 6 servings)

advance preparation

Refrigerate this soup and the chutney in separate covered containers for up to 2 days. Before serving, stir in vegetable stock or water to thin as desired.

TIPS

The two most common varieties of avocados are the Florida Fuerte, which has a smooth green skin and a relatively firm mild-flavored flesh, and the pebbly textured, almost-black California Hass. Because of their rich, buttery flavor and creamy, higher-fat flesh, Hass avocados are better for puréeing.

Some avocados require a few days of ripening after purchasing; place them in a loosely closed paper bag at room temperature for a day or two to speed up the process. Avocados yield to gentle pressure when ripe and ready to use; for puréeing, they should be quite ripe. Store ripe avocados in a plastic or paper bag in the refrigerator for up to 3 days. Once cut and exposed to air, avocado flesh discolors rapidly; to minimize this, coat the cut surfaces with citrus juice and add citrus juice to recipes calling for avocados.

To remove citrus zest, use a zester, which has a short, flat blade with a beveled end and 5 small holes. When drawn firmly over the skin of a citrus fruit, the tool removes thin strips of the colored zest. (Do not strip off the white pith beneath; it has a bitter flavor). Or, use a vegetable peeler to remove strips of the zest. Then use a knife to thinly slice the strips.

The qualities of an exceptional cook are akin to those of a successful tightrope walker: an abiding passion for the task, courage to go out on a limb, and an impeccable sense of balance.

—Bryan Miller

chunky gazpacho

Vegan recipe if sugar is substituted for honey

This thick and chunky soup can be a light meal in itself on a blistering hot day.
Serve it in chilled bowls and garnish with crispy croutons.

Combine the tomato sauce, vinegar, oil, and honey in a medium bowl. Stir in
all the remaining ingredients, except the croutons.

Refrigerate in a covered container until chilled, at least 3 hours, before serving. Taste and adjust the seasoning.

Garnish the servings with croutons.

advance preparation

This soup will keep for up to 5 days in a covered container in the
refrigerator. Before serving, stir in water or tomato juice to thin as desired.

TIPS

Extra-virgin olive oil is made from the first pressing of olives and contains only 1
percent acid or less. It is rich in flavor and is best reserved for uncooked dishes or for
drizzling into food at the end of cooking time. Avoid cooking with extra-virgin olive oil,
because the flavor breaks down at high temperatures.

   If you use olive oil regularly, keep it in a cool, dark place for up to 6 months. For longer
storage, refrigerate for up to 1 year. It will partially solidify at cold temperatures; bring it to
room temperature before using.

Look for small, thin cucumbers, which are less likely to be bitter. To seed them, cut
in half lengthwise, then starting at one end, scrape the seeds down the length of the
cucumber with the tip of a spoon or melon baller. If the skin is thick or waxed, peel the
cucumber before using. Long, slender European or English (hothouse) cucumbers are
nearly seedless, thinner skinned, and available year-round.

---

1   15-ounce can tomato sauce

2   tablespoons red wine vinegar

1   tablespoon extra-virgin olive oil *(see Tips)*

1   tablespoon honey

1   cucumber, seeded and coarsely chopped *(see Tips)*

1   tomato, cut into 1/2-inch dice

1/2   green bell pepper, seeded, deribbed, and coarsely chopped

1/2   red bell pepper, seeded, deribbed, and coarsely chopped

1   celery stalk, strings removed, coarsely chopped

2   tablespoons minced red onion, or to taste

2   cloves garlic, minced

1/4   teaspoon Tabasco sauce, or to taste

1/4   teaspoon freshly ground pepper, or to taste

~   salt to taste

~   Herbed Garlic Croutons *(page 150)* for garnish

Makes 4 cups (4 servings)

dessert soups

Whether fruity or even chocolaty, luscious dessert soups are an innovative finale to any meal. They also make easy snacks.

These may be prepared ahead, ready to serve when your guests are. Some of the soups are flavored with liqueur for a true adult treat. Serve them in fancy cups or wine goblets.

If you aren't up to a little magic occasionally, you shouldn't waste time trying to cook.
—Colette

berry-wine soup

Vegan recipe

Slightly tangy, ever so refreshing, and surprisingly simple to prepare, this crimson soup is an elegant way to enjoy juicy fresh summer berries. Serve it for dessert, or as a first course, accompanied with Rosemary Shortbread (page 158).

Combine all the ingredients, except the wine and garnish, in a medium saucepan; bring to a boil over medium-high heat.

Remove from the heat and let cool. Remove and discard the cinnamon stick and stir in the wine.

Refrigerate in a covered container until chilled, at least 4 hours. Garnish each serving with a lemon slice.

advance preparation

This soup will keep for up to 2 days in a covered container in the refrigerator.

variation

Substitute raspberry vinegar for the wine.

TIP

Because they don't travel well and do not ripen once picked, locally grown berries are your best choice. Remove any that are mushy or show signs of mold, and wash them just before using. Rinse berries gently in cool water and pat dry with paper towels.

1	cup cranberry juice cocktail
1	cup fresh raspberries *(see Tip)*
1	cup hulled and sliced fresh strawberries *(see Tip)*
1/2	cup fresh blueberries
1/4	cup pure maple syrup
1	cinnamon stick
~	pinch of ground cloves
1/4	cup dry red wine, preferably a fruity one, such as Zinfandel
~	thin lemon slices for garnish

strawberry-rhubarb soup with citrus sorbet

Tart rhubarb and sweet strawberries are naturally complementary. I like to make this in spring, when the first rhubarb is ready for picking, but at other times frozen rhubarb will do.

Combine all the ingredients, except the strawberries, sorbet, and garnish, in a medium saucepan. Bring to a boil over high heat. Reduce the heat; cover and simmer until the rhubarb is tender, about 12 minutes for fresh rhubarb, 5 minutes for frozen.

Drain the liquid by stirring it through a fine-meshed sieve over a medium bowl; discard the solids.

Transfer the liquid to a blender and add the strawberries; purée until smooth and creamy.

Refrigerate in a covered container until chilled, at least 4 hours, before serving.

To serve, ladle the soup into shallow bowls and add a small scoop of sorbet in the center of each serving. Garnish with lemon zest strips.

advance preparation

This soup will keep for up to 2 days in a covered container in the refrigerator.

TIPS

Field-grown rhubarb has red stalks and is more pronounced in flavor than the pink hothouse varieties. Because it is highly perishable, use fresh rhubarb as soon as possible; refrigerate it, tightly wrapped in a plastic bag, for up to 3 days. The leaves of rhubarb are toxic, so be sure to remove any before cooking the stalks.

Wrap vanilla beans tightly in plastic wrap, place them in an airtight jar, and refrigerate for up to 6 months. To use, slit the beans lengthwise down the center. You can scrape out the seeds to add directly to foods, such as ice creams and sauces, or the entire pod can be cooked in a mixture and removed before serving.

1	pound rhubarb (about 4 stalks) cut into 1-inch lengths *(see Tips)*
1	cup fresh orange juice
~	thin strips of zest of 1 orange *(see Tips, page 131)*
1/4	cup sugar
1	vanilla bean, halved lengthwise *(see Tips)*
1	cup hulled and sliced fresh strawberries
1	cup lemon or orange sorbet
~	thin strips of lemon zest for garnish *(see Tips, page 131)*

Makes 2 cups (4 servings)

fresh pink peach soup

Make this when peaches and strawberries are aromatic and at their ripe, juicy summer best. For a smooth, velvety texture, it's important that they be quite soft. Only fresh-squeezed orange and lemon juice will do. Add extra sugar, as needed, depending on the natural sweetness of the fruit and orange juice.

Purée all the ingredients, except the garnishes, in a blender until smooth. Taste and adjust the sweetening.

Refrigerate in a covered container until chilled, at least 3 hours, before serving. Garnish each serving with yogurt and a sprinkling of blueberries.

advance preparation

This soup is best when made a few hours before serving. It will keep for up to 2 days in a covered container in the refrigerator.

variation

Substitute 1 1/2 cups frozen peach wedges, thawed, for the fresh peaches.

TIPS

To squeeze more juice from citrus fruits, first bring them to room temperature or microwave chilled fruit (first pierce the fruit with a fork or knife) for 30 seconds on high.

Freshly grated whole nutmeg is more aromatic and flavorful than preground nutmeg. Use a nutmeg grater or a nutmeg grinder, which can be purchased in a gourmet shop. Whole nutmeg will keep its flavor for years if stored in a jar in your spice cabinet.

140

2	cups hulled and sliced fresh strawberries
2	peaches, pitted, peeled, and sliced
1/2	cup fresh orange juice *(see Tips)*
1/2	cup plain yogurt, plus more for garnish
3	tablespoons sugar, or to taste
1	tablespoon fresh lemon juice *(see Tips)*
1/8	teaspoon freshly grated nutmeg *(see Tips)*
~	fresh blueberries for garnish

Makes 4 cups (4 servings)

strawberry bonbon soup

Your best-loved fruit bonbon in a bowl, this soup is hard to beat. The chocolate sauce is speedy, but your jarred favorite from the supermarket will work just fine. For a festive presentation, serve in clear glass dessert bowls or martini glasses with a strawberry on each rim.

to make the soup

Purée all the ingredients in a blender until smooth. Adjust the sweetening to taste. Refrigerate in a covered container until chilled, at least 3 hours, before serving.

to make the chocolate sauce

Stir the chocolate and butter in a double boiler over simmering water (see Tips, page 143) until melted. Remove from the heat. Whisk in the maple syrup and cream until smooth. Serve immediately, or set aside and let cool.

To serve, drizzle a swirl of chocolate sauce over bowls of the chilled soup and garnish with fresh mint and strawberries.

advance preparation

Refrigerate this soup and the chocolate sauce in separate covered containers for up to 2 days. When chilled, the sauce will become firm; reheat in the microwave on high for about 30 seconds, or until softened; stir before using. Or, reheat, stirring constantly, in a double boiler over simmering water.

TIP

When buying maple syrup, look for the word *pure* on the label; others may be corn syrup with maple flavoring. Pure maple syrup is graded according to its color and flavor; the darker the color, the stronger the flavor. The lightest syrup is Grade A, called "fancy" in Vermont. It has the most delicate flavor and is the most expensive. Once opened, store maple syrup in the refrigerator, where it will keep for up to 1 year.

soup

2 cups hulled and sliced fresh strawberries

1 cup plain yogurt

1/4 cup red grape juice or sweet wine, such as Muscat

1 tablespoon sugar, or to taste

chocolate sauce

1 ounce unsweetened chocolate

1 teaspoon butter

3 tablespoons pure maple syrup *(see Tip)*

1 tablespoon heavy cream or half-and-half

~ sprigs of fresh mint and whole strawberries for garnish

141

Makes 2 cups (4 servings)

liquid chocolate with angel food croutons

This dessert soup was inspired by the almost-pudding-thick hot chocolate my son and I enjoyed in Spain. Prepare this as a special treat for your favorite chocolate-lover. Add Kahlúa for the adults.

to make the croutons

Preheat the oven to 400° F. Place the cake cubes in a single layer on an ungreased baking sheet. Toast for about 4 minutes, turning once, or until crisp and lightly browned on all sides but soft on the inside. (They will become firmer as they cool.)

to make the soup

Stir 1 3/4 cups of the milk and the chocolate together in a double boiler (see Tips) over simmering water. Stir occasionally until the chocolate is melted. Add the sugar and stir until dissolved.

Stir together the remaining 1/4 cup milk and the cornstarch in a small bowl until smooth. Add to the chocolate mixture, stirring constantly as it becomes glossy and smooth and thickens to cake-batter consistency, about 3 minutes.

Add the Kahlúa (if using), butter, vanilla, cinnamon, and salt; stir until the butter melts. Taste and adjust the flavoring.

Serve the soup warm, topped with the croutons.

croutons

2   cups angel food cake cut into 1/2-inch cubes

soup

2   cups milk (preferably whole or 2 percent)

3   ounces semisweet chocolate, coarsely chopped (see Tips)

2   tablespoons sugar

2   tablespoons cornstarch

1/4   cup Kahlúa (optional)

1   teaspoon unsalted butter

1   teaspoon pure vanilla extract

~   scant pinch of ground cinnamon, or to taste

~   pinch of salt, or to taste

Makes 2 cups (4 servings)

advance preparation

This soup will keep for up to 3 days in a covered container in the refrigerator. To reheat, stir gently over medium heat. Store the croutons for up to 2 days in a tightly covered tin at room temperature.

TIPS

Chocolate should be stored, tightly wrapped, in a cool, dry place, where it will keep for more than 1 year. If it becomes mottled with a light-gray film (known as bloom), it will not affect the way chocolate performs or tastes.

A double boiler is a double pan, with one sitting part way inside the other. The lower pot is used to hold simmering water, which gently heats the mixture in the top pot. Adjust the level of the water so it does not touch the bottom of the top pan. Use a double boiler to cook heat-sensitive foods, such as custards, delicate sauces, and chocolate. If you don't have a double boiler, use a stainless-steel bowl set over a saucepan of simmering water.

My favorite word is "chocolate."
It's the most delicious word I know.
The word—if I read it or write it
or say it—tastes just great to me.
—Maida Heatter

gingered pear soup

Vegan recipe

I like the aromas and flavors of this light, simple dessert best when it is served warm, but if you prefer, serve warm soup over room-temperature pears or chill both components. Buttery-rich Rosemary Shortbread (page 158) is a lovely accompaniment.

to poach the pears

Combine the water, wine, sugar, orange slices, and cloves in a medium saucepan. Bring to a boil over high heat. Reduce the heat; simmer for 5 minutes. Add the pears; simmer, turning occasionally, until they are tender, 10 to 15 minutes.

to make the soup

Wrap the ginger, bay leaf, cinnamon stick, peppercorns, aniseed, and clove in a cheesecloth square and tie with kitchen twine (see Tips, page 33). Pour the pear nectar into a small saucepan; add the cheesecloth bag. Bring to a boil over high heat. Reduce the heat; cover and simmer for 15 minutes. Taste and let the broth steep if you want a stronger spice flavor.

To serve, place a pear upright in the center of a dessert bowl. (Even the bottom of the pear if necessary, so it will stand up straight.) Ladle the soup into the bowl. Insert a mint sprig into the center of the pear.

continued . . .

pears

1½	cups water
¾	cup sweet white wine, such as Sauternes or sweet Riesling
⅓	cup sugar
2	¼-inch-thick orange slices
4	whole cloves
4	Bosc, Bartlett, or Forelle pears, cored and peeled *(see Tips, page 146)*

soup

3	½-inch-thick fresh ginger slices
1	bay leaf
1	cinnamon stick
1	teaspoon black peppercorns
¼	teaspoon aniseed, or 2 star anise pods *(see Tips, page 146)*
1	whole clove
2	cups pear nectar
~	sprigs of fresh mint for garnish

Makes 2 cups (4 servings)

advance preparation

This soup and the pears will keep for up to 1 day in separate covered containers in the refrigerator.

variation

If you prefer, leave the stems intact when coring the pears.

TIPS

Most pears develop a better flavor and smoother texture when ripened off the tree, so buy them while they are firm and ripen them for 2 to 7 days on your kitchen counter in a loosely closed paper bag or a covered fruit-ripening bowl. To speed ripening, add an apple or banana to the container. Because they ripen from the inside out, most pears do not show ripeness with a color change. Pears used for cooking or baking should be slightly underripe. For eating, the flesh should give slightly to gentle pressure. Once ripe, refrigerate unwashed pears in a plastic or paper bag for up to 3 days.

Aniseed, a member of the parsley family, has a distinctive, sweet licorice flavor. Star anise, commonly used in Asian cuisines, is the star-shaped dark brown pod of a small evergreen tree in the magnolia family. It, too, has a licorice flavor.

A good cook is like a sorceress who dispenses happiness.
—Elsa Schiaparelli

brandied pumpkin panna cotta soup

1   15-ounce can
      pumpkin purée

1   cup heavy cream,
      half-and-half, or milk

1/2   cup milk

1/2   cup sugar

1/4   cup apricot brandy

~   crème fraîche *(see Tip)*,
      thinned with milk, and
      crumbled gingersnaps
      for garnish

Panna cotta is Italian for "cooked cream." Traditionally, it is a light custard. Here, it's flavored with pumpkin and apricot brandy and served as a dessert soup.

Purée the pumpkin, cream, milk, and sugar in a blender. Stir in the brandy.

Refrigerate in a covered container until chilled, about 3 hours, before serving. (The mixture will thicken.)

Serve garnished with swirls of crème fraîche and crumbled gingersnaps.

advance preparation

This soup will keep for up to 2 days in a covered container in the refrigerator.

TIP

Crème fraîche is a thickened cream, sold in the dairy section of gourmet markets and some supermarkets. It's smooth and rich, with a tangy and slightly nutty flavor. As a substitute, whisk together equal amounts of sour cream and heavy cream until thickened.

147

Makes 3 1/2 cups (6 servings)

garnishes and accompaniments

Here are some little extras that will add flavor and crunch to your soup courses. They are quick to prepare and add a personal touch. In lieu of ordinary bread try Sun-Dried Tomato–Goat Cheese Bruschetta (page 156). Instead of store-bought crackers, try Gruyère Cheese Crisps (page 162), Toasted Pita Triangles (page 159), or mouthwatering Rosemary Shortbread (page 158).

Herbed Garlic Croutons (page 150) and Buttered Croutons (page 151) are great ways to use leftover bread, and they are better than the packaged ones any day.

Many excellent artisan breads are now available. With Italian-inspired soups, serve a crusty Italian loaf with Basil Pesto Butter (page 155). And add flair by serving your soup in Roasted Acorn Squash Soup Bowls (page 152).

Remember, too, that your table setting adds to the dining experience; select plates, bowls, silverware, and a bread basket that reflect your personality and sense of style.

herbed garlic croutons

2 tablespoons olive oil

2 cloves garlic, minced *(see Tip)*

1/2 teaspoon dried basil

1/2 teaspoon dried oregano

2 slices whole-wheat bread, cut into 1/2-inch cubes (2 cups)

Vegan recipe, depending on ingredients in bread (check package label)

Great on warm Roasted Butternut Squash Soup (page 34) or chilled Chunky Gazpacho (page 132), these crunchy rustic croutons add flavor and texture.

Heat the oil in a large skillet over medium heat. Add the garlic, basil, and oregano; cook, stirring constantly, until the garlic is softened, about 30 seconds.

Add the bread cubes and stir constantly until lightly browned and crisp, 5 to 10 minutes, depending on the moistness of the bread. Transfer to a plate to cool.

advance preparation

These croutons will keep for up to 2 days in a tightly covered tin at room temperature. If stored in a plastic container, they'll become soggy. To recrisp, spread them on a baking sheet and heat in a preheated 350° F oven for about 5 minutes.

TIP

Throughout the centuries, garlic, a member of the lily family, has flavored soups, stews, and bread, and been taken for any number of ailments, from toothaches to infertility. Look for plump, fresh bulbs that have not sprouted. Store them unwrapped in a cool, dark place; avoid refrigeration, which promotes rotting. Do not use powdered, dried, or jarred garlic if a recipe calls for fresh.

The more fresh garlic is cooked, the milder it becomes. Roasting produces a mild, sweet, and nutty flavor; boiling, a mild flavor; sautéing, a moderately strong flavor with more bite than boiled garlic but with less intensity than raw garlic.

There are five elements: earth, air, fire, water, and garlic.

—Louis Diat

Makes 2 cups

buttered croutons

Shaped croutons will add whimsy to your soups and make your guests smile. Use cookie cutters to cut bread slices into circles, moons, stars, hearts, diamonds, or whatever suits your fancy or theme.

Slice off the crusts and cut the bread into shapes using cookie cutters. Combine the cheese, paprika, and salt into a small brown paper bag or heavy-duty plastic container with a lid. Shake to blend. Set aside.

Melt the butter with the oil in a medium skillet over medium-high heat. When a drop of water sizzles when sprinkled into the pan, add the bread shapes. Use tongs to turn them and fry until they are evenly browned, 3 to 4 minutes per side. Drain the croutons on a paper towel–lined plate.

While the croutons are still hot, drop them into the paper bag or plastic container. Close the bag or cover the container and shake until the croutons are evenly coated.

advance preparation

These croutons will keep for up to 2 days in a tightly closed tin at room temperature.

Dining is and always was a great artistic opportunity.
—Frank Lloyd Wright

2–3 thin slices day-old white or whole-wheat bread

2 tablespoons freshly grated (finely) Parmesan cheese

1/4 teaspoon sweet paprika, preferably Hungarian

~ dash of salt

2 tablespoons unsalted butter

3 tablespoons olive oil

Yield is variable

roasted acorn squash soup bowls

1 large acorn squash *(see Tip)*

~ canola or olive oil for brushing

~ salt for sprinkling

~ warm soup for serving

Vegan recipe

Roasted acorn squash looks lovely and tastes fabulous when scooped up with spoonfuls of soup, such as Pumpkin Stew (page 96), Greek Spinach and Orzo Soup (page 89), or Arborio Rice Soup (page 62).

Preheat the oven to 375° F. Cut the acorn squash in half horizontally. Scoop out the seeds and discard. Use a spoon to remove any strings and to smooth out the insides. Cut a very thin slice off the bottoms to make a stable base. Brush the insides and tops with oil and sprinkle lightly with salt.

Place the squash halves, cut-side down, in a lightly oiled baking pan. Pierce the skin in several places with a fork. Bake for about 45 minutes, or until the flesh is fork tender.

Place the roasted squash on a plate or set in a soup bowl. Fill with warm soup and serve immediately.

variations

~ Substitute other similar-sized squash for acorn squash, such as Carnival Squash, which has an orange, green, and yellow skin and a sweet, bright orange flesh.

~ The soup bowls can be baked in the microwave. Prepare the squash as for oven roasting. Place the squash halves, cut-side down, in a microwave-proof dish. Pierce the skin in several places with a fork. Add ¼ cup water. Microwave on high for 8 to 10 minutes, or until the flesh is fork tender.

TIP

Though it is available year-round, winter squash is best from early fall through the winter months. When selecting winter squash such as acorn squash, look for a firm squash that feels heavy for its size and has no soft spots. Winter squash does not require refrigeration; store it in a cool, dark, dry, and well-ventilated place for up to 1 month.

2 bowls per squash

basil pesto

Vegan recipe

I always have pesto on hand. At the end of the growing season, I pinch the leaves from my basil plants to make this aromatic blend. Basil pesto can add lots of flavor to soups. It can also be mixed with butter for a flavorful spread for bread (facing page) or used to make bruschetta (page 157).

Process all the ingredients in a food processor until coarsely puréed. Using a rubber spatula, scrape down the sides as needed.

advance preparation

This pesto will keep for up to 1 week in a covered container in the refrigerator; pour a thin film of olive oil on top of the pesto to prevent discoloration. For longer storage, spoon the mixture, in 2-tablespoon quantities, into foil-lined mini-muffin tins; cover tightly with aluminum foil and freeze. Once frozen, remove the foil-wrapped packets and store for up to 3 months in a freezer bag. To use, thaw in the refrigerator overnight or remove from the foil and thaw quickly in a microwave.

TIP

To store fresh herbs, wrap the stem ends in a moist paper towel and refrigerate in a sealed plastic bag. Or, place the bunch, stems down, in a glass of water and cover with a plastic bag, securing the bag to the glass with a rubber band; change the water every 2 days. With proper storage, fresh herbs will last for about 5 days, but for the best flavor, use them within 2 or 3 days. Just before using, wash fresh herbs in cool water, then dry them with paper towels or in a salad spinner.

1½ cups lightly packed fresh basil leaves *(see Tip)*

¼ cup pine nuts

3 tablespoons extra-virgin olive oil

2 cloves garlic, minced

¼ teaspoon freshly ground pepper

~ dash of salt

Makes ½ cup

basil pesto butter

4 tablespoons unsalted butter at room temperature *(see Tip)*

1/4 cup Basil Pesto *(facing page)*

~ salt and freshly ground pepper to taste

This mixture of unsalted butter and basil pesto makes a lovely spread on crusty artisan bread to accompany your soups.

Stir together the butter and pesto in a small bowl until smooth; season to taste. Transfer to a small serving bowl.

Serve immediately or cover and refrigerate until firmer.

advance preparation

This spread will keep for up to 1 week in a covered container in the refrigerator.

TIP

Unsalted butter is labeled as such. Because it contains no salt, which acts as a preservative, it is more perishable than salted butter and may be found in the freezer section of some supermarkets. At home, wrap it tightly in aluminum foil or plastic wrap and freeze for up to 6 months.

Honest bread is very well—it's the butter
that makes the temptation.

—Douglas Jerrold

155

Makes 1/3 cup

sun-dried tomato–goat cheese bruschetta

These warm open-faced sandwiches are a staple in Italy. The term comes from the Italian *bruscare,* meaning "to roast over coals," and the traditional garlic bread is made by rubbing slices of toasted bread with garlic cloves, then drizzling the bread with extra-virgin oil and holding over an open fire. It can be topped with a wide variety of ingredients or simply sprinkled with coarse salt and pepper.

156

Position the oven rack to 4 to 5 inches from the broiler heating element; preheat the broiler.

Arrange the bread slices in a single layer on a baking sheet. Lightly toast under the broiler, about 1 minute per side. The bread should be golden brown and crisp on the outside, chewy and soft on the inside.

Rub one side of each warm slice with cut garlic; the more you rub, the stronger the flavor.

Stir together the plum tomato, sun-dried tomatoes, olive oil, basil, pepper, and salt in a small bowl.

Spread the bread slices with the goat cheese and top with the tomato mixture; sprinkle with Parmesan cheese.

Broil until the cheese is melted, about 1 1/2 minutes. Serve warm or at room temperature.

8	1/2–to 3/4-inch slices rustic Italian bread or French baguette cut on an extreme diagonal (day-old is fine)
~	halved garlic cloves for rubbing
1	plum tomato, cut into 1/4-inch dice *(see Tips)*
2	tablespoons minced oil-packed sun-dried tomatoes, drained *(see Tips)*
1	teaspoon extra-virgin olive oil (or you can use some of the drained oil from the sun-dried tomatoes)
2	tablespoons minced fresh basil
1/4	teaspoon freshly ground pepper, or to taste
~	dash of salt, or to taste
3	tablespoons fresh white goat cheese *(chèvre; see Tip, page 80)*
3	tablespoons freshly grated Parmesan cheese

Makes 4 servings

advance preparation

The bread can be toasted early in the day. The tomato topping will keep for up to 1 day in a covered container in the refrigerator. Bring the topping to room temperature; assemble and broil the bruschetta just before serving.

variation

Rather than rubbing the toasted bread with garlic, spread it with Basil Pesto (page 154). Omit the basil in the tomato topping.

TIPS

Plum, or Roma, tomatoes have thick, meaty walls, small seeds, little juice, and a rich, sweet flavor. They are the best choice for recipes that benefit from less juicy tomatoes that retain their shape after being chopped or sliced.

For this recipe, use a jar of oil-packed sun-dried tomatoes. Drain off the excess oil before using. (The oil can be saved, refrigerated, and used in recipes calling for olive oil, especially recipes with tomatoes as an ingredient.) Refrigerate the jar of tomatoes for up to 2 weeks after opening.

Bread is like dresses, hats, or shoes—
in other words, essential.
—Emily Post

rosemary shortbread

This tender and crispy shortbread makes a buttery-rich and not-too-sweet accompaniment to light soups. I think it's especially enjoyable with Berry-Wine Soup (page 137) and Gingered Pear Soup (page 144), and I know my guests agree.

Use an electric mixer to combine the butter and sugar in a medium bowl; mix on low speed just until combined and not fluffy, about 30 seconds. Add the flour and salt all at once; mix on low speed just until the mixture barely holds together, about 30 seconds. Add the rosemary, beating briefly until evenly combined. (The dough will look slightly lumpy.)

Using the back of a measuring cup or spoon, press the dough into a 9-inch square pan. Cover with plastic wrap and refrigerate for at least 1 hour, or until fairly firm.

When ready to bake, preheat the oven to 300° F. Pierce the dough several places with a fork. Bake for about 30 minutes, or until the shortbread is just firm but not at all brown. (If it browns, it will be overbaked.) Let cool in the pan on a wire rack.

To serve, cut the shortbread into squares, strips, or diamond shapes. Carefully remove them from the pan with a small metal spatula. (The shortbread is fragile and breaks easily.)

advance preparation

Store this shortbread in the pan; cover lightly and refrigerate or keep at room temperature for up to 2 days.

½   cup (1 stick) unsalted butter at room temperature

¼   cup sugar

1¼ cups all-purpose flour, sifted

~   pinch of salt

1   tablespoon minced fresh (fresh is essential) rosemary
(see Tips, page 115)

Makes 1 shortbread (about 36 pieces)

toasted pita triangles

2   6-inch white or whole-wheat pita pocket breads

2   tablespoons olive oil or melted unsalted butter

1   teaspoon dried oregano
(see Tip)

1/4   cup freshly grated Parmesan cheese

Vegan recipe if cooked in oil, not butter (also depending on ingredients in pitas—check label)

Serve these in place of store-bought crackers. They are crisp, appetizing, and addictive.

Position the oven rack 4 to 5 inches from the broiler heating element; preheat the broiler.

Slice the pita breads in half horizontally. Place the halves on a baking sheet, rough-side up. Using a pastry brush, lightly spread them with olive oil, then sprinkle with the oregano and Parmesan cheese. Use kitchen shears to cut each pita half into 6 triangles.

Place the triangles in a single layer on a baking sheet and broil until they are lightly browned and the cheese is melted, about 2 minutes. Watch closely! (The triangles will become crisper as they cool.)

advance preparation

Pita triangles are best when prepared just before serving; serve warm or at room temperature. Refrigerate extras for up to 2 days in a covered container. To recrisp, spread them on a baking sheet and heat in a preheated 350° F oven for about 5 minutes.

variation

Substitute other dried herbs, such as basil or tarragon, for the oregano.

TIP

When stored in a tightly closed tin or glass container in a dark, dry place, dried herbs will remain flavorful for about 1 year; it's a good idea to date them. They should resemble the color they were when fresh and should not be dull or brownish-green.

To get the most flavor out of dried herbs, crumble them between your fingers to release the aromatic oil as you add them to your recipes.

159

Makes 24

cheese sticks

Flaky, crisp, and cheesy, these are simple to make and rustic pretty. If you haven't worked with puff pastry before, begin by reading the tip on page 33.

Preheat the oven to 400° F. Line a baking sheet with aluminum foil. Lightly beat the egg in a small bowl. Combine the cheeses, sesame seeds, paprika, oregano, thyme, and pepper in another small bowl.

Unroll the puff pastry on a lightly floured board, one long side toward you. Using a pastry brush, brush the top side with the egg. Sprinkle with half of the cheese mixture. Fold the bottom half of the dough over the cheese. Using a rolling pin, roll gently away from you to make the pastry layers stick together and to spread the dough into a 10-by-8-inch rectangle. Brush the top surface with the egg and sprinkle with the remaining cheese mixture.

Using a sharp knife or pizza wheel, cut the pastry vertically into twenty 1/2-inch-wide strips. Twist each about 4 times into spirals as you place it on a baking sheet, pressing the ends down to hold the strip in place. Position the strips at least 1 inch apart.

Bake for about 15 minutes, or until golden brown. Use a spatula to remove the sticks from the baking sheet. Serve warm, or let cool on a wire rack.

1 egg

1/2 cup freshly grated (finely) Parmesan cheese

1/2 cup finely grated sharp Cheddar cheese

2 tablespoons toasted sesame seeds *(see Tips)*

1 teaspoon sweet paprika, preferably Hungarian *(see Tips)*

1 teaspoon dried oregano

1 teaspoon dried thyme

1/2 teaspoon ground pepper

1 frozen puff pastry sheet (8 to 10 ounces), thawed

Makes 20

advance preparation

The unbaked cheese sticks can be covered with plastic wrap and refrigerated for up to 8 hours. Or, wrap them tightly in aluminum foil and freeze for up to 1 month; defrost before baking. These are best when served fresh from the oven but can be kept for up to 1 day in a tightly covered container at room temperature.

TIPS

Toasting gives sesame seeds a slightly crisp texture and a nutty flavor. Put the seeds in a dry skillet over medium-high heat and toss or stir constantly until they are lightly browned, about 3 to 5 minutes. Immediately transfer the seeds to a bowl. It takes the same amount of time to toast 1 tablespoon or 1/2 cup, so toast extra seeds, store them in an airtight container, and refrigerate or freeze for up to 6 months.

Paprika is made from ground dried sweet red peppers. Most paprika comes from Spain, South America, California, or Hungary; the Hungarian variety is considered by many to be the best. Hungarian paprika comes in three levels of heat: mild (also called "sweet"), hot, and exceptionally hot. To preserve its color and flavor, paprika should be stored in a cool, dark place for no longer than 6 months.

gruyère cheese crisps

These delicate cheese wafers are a light and crispy soup accompaniment, speedy and simple, best when made just before serving.

162

Preheat the oven to 350° F. Line a baking sheet with parchment paper (see Tips).

Cut the cheese into 1/4-inch-thick slices, then into 1 1/2-by-1-inch rectangles. Place them about 2 inches apart (they will spread and become round as they bake) on the prepared baking sheet. Sprinkle each piece of cheese with some of the pecans.

Bake for about 12 minutes, or until bubbly and very lightly browned.

Place the baking sheet on a wire rack and let the cheese crisps cool. Using a metal spatula, transfer the crisps to a plate lined with a paper towel to absorb any excess oil.

advance preparation

These cheese crisps are best when made the day of serving; cover lightly and store at room temperature. For longer storage, refrigerate for up to 2 days in a covered container.

TIPS

Gruyère cheese is a cow's milk cheese with a rich, sweet, and nutty flavor and a pale yellow color. Buy the aged Swiss or French variety that is cut into wedges from large wheels rather than processed Gruyère.

Parchment paper is a grease- and moisture-resistant paper that can be used to line baking pans, to wrap foods that are to be baked *en papillote,* and to make disposable pastry bags. Parchment paper is available in kitchen supply stores and most super-markets.

Makes 24

~ Extra-virgin olive oil
~ Whole fresh sage leaves
~ Fine salt for sprinkling

fried sage

Vegan recipe

Sage leaves may sizzle when added to the hot oil but won't splatter if they're patted dry. They make an attractive and tasty garnish.

Pour ¹/2 inch oil into a small saucepan or skillet and heat over medium-high heat. When a drop of water sizzles when sprinkled into the pan, add the sage leaves. Fry for about 15 seconds, turning occasionally with a slotted spoon or tongs. (Don't let the leaves brown, or they'll become bitter.)

Transfer the leaves to a paper towel–lined plate. The leaves will become crisp as they cool. Sprinkle lightly with fine-textured salt.

advance preparation

Fried sage will keep for up to 2 days in a tightly closed container at room temperature.

All's well that ends with a good meal.
—Arnold Lobel

Yield is variable

index

table of equivalents

The exact equivalents in the following tables have been rounded for convenience.

liquid and dry measures

U.S.		METRIC	
1/4	teaspoon	1.25	milliliters
1/2	teaspoon	2.5	milliliters
1	teaspoon	5	milliliters
1	tablespoon *(3 teaspoons)*	15	milliliters
1	fluid ounce *(2 tablespoons)*	30	milliliters
1/4	cup	60	milliliters
1/3	cup	80	milliliters
1	cup	240	milliliters
1	pint *(2 cups)*	480	milliliters
1	quart *(4 cups, 32 ounces)*	960	milliliters
1	gallon *(4 quarts)*	3.84	liters
1	ounce *(by weight)*	28	grams
1	pound	454	grams
2.2	pounds	1	kilogram

oven temperatures

FAHRENHEIT	CELSIUS	GAS
250	120	1/2
275	140	1
300	150	2
325	160	3
350	180	4
375	190	5
400	200	6
425	220	7
450	230	8
475	240	9
500	260	10

length measures

U.S.		METRIC	
1/8	inch	3	millimeters
1/4	inch	6	millimeters
1/2	inch	12	millimeters
1	inch	2.5	centimeters